MESOAMERICAN HISTORY & MYTHOLOGY

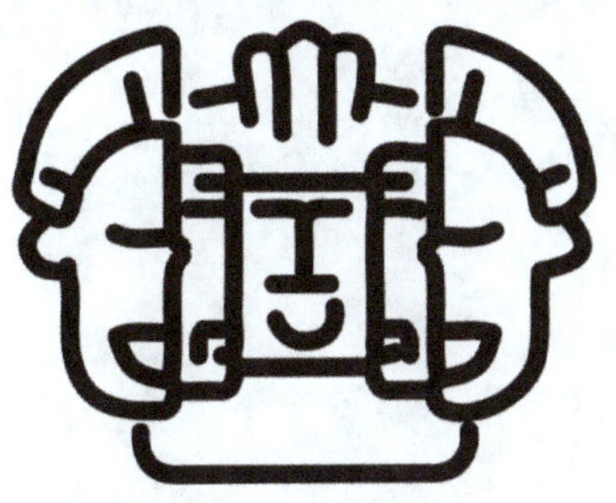

Aztec, Inca, Maya, Toltec, Zapotec & Central American Myths, Legends, Mysteries & History Uncovered

HISTORY BROUGHT ALIVE

FREE BONUS FROM HBA: EBOOK BUNDLE

Greetings!

First of all, thank you for reading our books. As fellow passionate readers of History and Mythology, we aim to create the very best books for our readers.

Now, we invite you to join our VIP list. As a welcome gift, we offer the History & Mythology Ebook Bundle below for free. Plus you can be the first to receive new books and exclusives! Remember it's 100% free to join.

Simply scan the QR code to join.

FREE DOWNLOAD

<u>Keep up to date with us on:</u>

YouTube: History Brought Alive

Facebook: History Brought Alive

<u>www.historybroughtalive.com</u>

CONTENTS

INTRODUCTION

What You Will Find Inside This Book: A Promise

Through this book, you'll discover the intricate world of the great civilizations that once inhabited what we now know as Mesoamerica. You'll learn about their history, their organization, and their mythology which will allow you to take a look at the world as they saw it. A fascinating world which will now be open to you, explained in a clear, easily understandable, and fascinating way.

Once you will have finished reading this book, you will have gained an understanding of how the aboriginal Mesoamerican civilizations viewed the world. You will understand what world the Spanish conquerors found when they arrived in the Americas, and what aspects of that world are still present in our modern day, even if they have changed with time.

This understanding will be very useful

because it will help you to visualize how these civilizations, active all those centuries ago, and their clash with the European worldview that the Spaniards brought with them, helped shape the Mesoamerican region into what it is today. After all, the world we live in today is but the result of history: the present is the result of the past. Understanding the past, therefore, will help us greatly to understand the present. So if you wish to understand the culture of the Mesoamerican region and the way it is today, this book is a great place to start.

The study of religion and mythology is particularly useful in this regard, because the myths and religious beliefs of a certain culture clearly show us the way that people view the world. This includes what is important to them, what is considered sacred, and how they try to answer the question that the physical world doesn't seem to have an answer for. These core beliefs permeate everyday life: the way the cities are organized, the relationship between humans and nature, and the rituals that took place. That's why this book will teach the reader, not only about aboriginal Mesoamerican mythology and religion, but also about their architecture, social organization, and more.

Before You Start Reading

A few words before the start of the learning journey and about what makes this book, and all books by History Brought Alive, the best in their category. The difference, the characteristic that makes our books unique, is the deep immersion experience they can provide the reader into the topic the book covers. A deep immersion that makes all the difference when it comes to the experience of reading a book and the learning experience that the reader may have when reading it that is further enhanced by the engaging, easy-to-understand way in which the material is presented.

Perhaps one of the most difficult aspects of trying to learn about a civilization that no longer exists, or that survives only through native descendants but has lost some key cultural aspects through the years, is the simple fact that their reality is not, exactly, our own reality. When we learn about a civilization like this, we must learn to view the world with completely different eyes. The eyes of someone that doesn't view or experience life in the same way we do, and who doesn't even live in the same world we live in, in the sense that the world today is vastly different from what it was centuries, or even millennia ago. It is very important to try and adopt this attitude as it is the best, and perhaps the only, way to really grasp the population that we are trying to learn about.

This immersion, in turn, is important, because the world as we know it is the result of the world as it was. When we learn about the past, we are actually going deep into what makes our reality what it is—the little bricks that have built it. By immersing ourselves and trying to see the world through the eyes of the civilization we're studying, we can really make that world our own. We can somehow identify with what we're learning and that helps to make for a better learning experience. We see the facts, the places, the beliefs, and rituals in their proper context and therefore are able to learn their true meaning because that meaning was rooted in the context in which the ritual was practiced, the belief held, or the city constructed.

Of course, all of this is made easy—or on the contrary, unnecessarily complex—by the material one uses to learn about the civilization one is interested in. That's why an informative book is so important! This book will provide you with the highly subversive experience you need in order to really feel you know and understand the subject matter. It will help you get a chance to actually be able to visualize what the world felt like for an Olmec, an Aztec, or a Maya. By doing that, this book will prove to be the best source of information about the subject of Mesoamerican history, religion, and mythology that you could possibly choose to study.

This is not only a promise made by this book, but by every book by History Brought Alive. Through that immersive experience, no matter what little corner of history you're exploring, History Brought Alive books really position you in the time and place where the action took place, giving you a front row seat to see our world being shaped into its current status.

So don't wait any longer! Don't waste more time with sources that do not bring you any magic. Choose History Brought Alive and have the best, most enriching learning experience you can have! You will find all the magic of the great Mesoamerican civilizations within these pages. If you wish to learn about more civilizations with all the quality of History Brought Alive, there are many other great book topics in our repertoire Ranging from Mythology for Kids, the Roman Empire, to the History of Asia, and many more! Make sure you check out these and other books by History Brought Alive, and start building up your history library today!

CHAPTER 1
MESOAMERICA: LOCATION, TIMELINE, SIMILARITIES AND DIFERRENCES BETWEEN DIFFERENT MESOAMERICAN CULTURES

What Do We Mean When We Say "Mesoamerica"? A Complex Concept

Let us start our journey through Mesoamerican history and religion by defining what Mesoamerica actually is. What do we mean when we use the term "Mesoamerica"? Well, "Mesoamerica" was coined in 1943 by anthropologist, Paul Kirchhoff, and it's used to define a geographical area between northern Mexico and the Gulf of Nicoya in Costa Rica. This corresponds to the middle segment of the American continent, Mexico being in North America and Costa Rica being in Central America. In fact, the word "Mesoamerica" means "Middle America", deriving from the

Greek word for middle, "mesos".

This being said, the geographical aspect is not the most important one when it comes to defining Mesomerica as a concept. This is defined as a common cultural area much more than just a geographical one. There are certain common cultural traits that unite this region into one unity. Language, religion (including ceremonies and activities partaking to religion), buildings such as pyramids, the use of stones to pave the roads and to build in general, among other traits, are more or less shared by the different cultures of this region.

Kirchhoff's definition is not the only one that has been used; but other definitions still base themselves on the idea of certain cultural traits. American anthropologist, Kroeber, for example, bases his definition on the use of the permuting calendar, while archaeologist Gordon Willey, anthropologist Gordon Eckholm, and archaeologist René Milton—authors of The Patterns of Farming Life and Civilization—consider traits such as a sedentary village life, agricultural practices, and (possibly) the creation of pottery.

As will become apparent throughout this book, there are many commonalities between the different Mesoamerican people. They share many aspects of their world views, rituals, and other cultural traits. That's why we can, for example, talk about the Mayan calendar, and find out it is surprisingly similar to the Zapotec ritual calendar. This will happen in various instances, and it is to be expected due to these factions all being part of the same region, not only in a geographical sense, but also in a cultural one.

It must also be said that the Incas, the last great civilization you will learn about in this book, lived in South America. Geographically, South America is not a part of Mesoamerica as we have conceptualized it; therefore, we could say that the Incas are not actually Mesoamerican, also on a cultural level. But, they were one of the great civilizations of the Americas, along with all the Mesoamerican ones, and therefore deserve a place in this book.

How Does Culture Change? Ideas for Mesoamerica

Of course, there are nuances to this idea, which makes our concept all the more complicated. For example, we could ask ourselves how does a certain cultural trait, such as agricultural practices, expand its area of ocurrence? We could say it expands, meaning it starts in a certain area and then gets adopted in other areas or places, in an outward fashion starting from the "nuclear area". Then we could find the trait later in these new areas other than in the "nuclear area". But examples such as maize agriculture or gold metallurgy go in different directions to this: diffusion is not all that happens.

Some archaeologists have used terms such as "frontiers" to try and explain the phenomenon of different cultural areas sharing certain traits from one to the other even if none of them appear to be clearly dominant over the other. In this model, the movement of cultural evolution is different from the idea of diffusion. In fact, the idea of "frontier" was first applied to the case of North America and the European conquest, a moment in which North American culture began to change. But this change went in a clear direction, whereas in Mesoamerica there was no such clear path, but rather a back and forth cultural movement. There is also the "buffer" theory, that derives from the "frontier" one: that of a "buffer zone", a sort of "mixed" middle ground between two distinct cultural zones. Central America could then be considered a buffer between Mesoamerica and South America.

Some experts, starting with Caldwell in

1964, prefer another theory and view Mesoamerica as an interactive sphere, where different groups interact with each other in a certain area—for example, by trading. This serves as an alternative explanation to diffusion.

Other approaches to the study of ancient civilizations include culture history and cultural evolution. When an archaeologist works through the lens of culture history, he or she is focusing their research on the idea that, whatever people do, they do it based on their own set of values, which are transmitted by one's culture. Therefore, by studying the actions of a certain civilization, and what happened as they came into contact with other people, a culture historian may develop an idea of what properly identified that group or civilization as such.

When an archaeologist uses the cultural evolution approach instead, he or she recognizes the fact that cultures change continually. Of course cultures are very complex systems and they have several components, from individuals to societies. When studying how societies change, experts must consider all of these different factors and their evolution is not always clear-cut. Some may simply stay the same, some may change with time, and some may even merge, or combine with each other. This makes working with cultural evolution a bit tricky, but an answer to the question of what these cultures were and how they evolved and changed may be achieved by paying close attention to how the people interacted with their environment, how they used the resources available to them, or what their political and social organization was like.

The other difficulty we can find with cultural evolution, is that culture doesn't change or evolve in a one-directional, easy-to-follow way. Instead, it jumps from one state of affairs to the next, sometimes entering a most complex state and sometimes quite the opposite. There is never a "logical next step" of cultural evolution that the archaeologist studying a certain culture or civilization may predict and look for, because culture can go in all sorts of different—and sometimes surprising—directions.

Of course, every one of these alternative explanations has its strengths and its weaknesses. They simply come to show the richness and complexity of the interactions and relationships between these different groups of people.

This complexity, in turn, is what makes studying these cultures all the more fascinating and challenging. In order to get as accurate a story as possible, archaeologists have been working since the 1950s studying "settlement patterns", which means trying to map out the whole site of a given city, from the ceremonial buildings that constituted the main area of the city to the habitational portion in the outskirts. The idea is to work with information partaking to whole societal groups, and not only isolated communities. This type of research has been done in places such as the Valley of Mexico and the Valley of Oaxaca.

If the reader should be interested in viewing a map of the Mesoamerican region, there is a rather good one in Ancient Mesoamerica: A Comparison of Change in Three Regions by Richard Blaton et al.

Basic Timeline of Mesoamerican History

It is, of course, hard to precisely determine when the first human population arrived and settled itself in Mesoamerica and its surrounding areas, as it may be difficult to really pinpoint any historical era with total precision.

It is believed, in light of what we currently know on the subject, that the earliest humans in the area date from 15,000 B.C.E. at the latest, with findings from the Southern Cone (the southmost part of South America) dating the earliest human presence around 12,000 B.C.E. We will fix the first period, which we can call the Paleoindian Period, between around 35,000 and 10,000, or 7,000 B.C.E. It is possible that humans crossed from Siberia to Alaska—to use today's geographical terms—via the Bering land bridge which connected both. This took several hundred years of sporadic crossings of human groups (Adams, R. E., & MacLeod, M. J. (Eds.), 2000).

After this first period comes the Archaic period, from around 8,000 or 7,000 B.C.E. to 1,500 B.C.E, a period in which human groups became more settled and transitioned from being hunters and gatherers to creating villages. There were agricultural villages all around Mesoamerica by 1,500 B.C.E. During this period the human population grew considerably and different groups within the region became increasingly different from each other as they could move less easily, and thus became each circumscribed to another particular area.

Within the pre-classic period, from 1,500 B.C.E. to approximately 150 C.E, cultures such as the Olmecs—which we will discuss in our next chapter—began to appear. By the end of this period, many of the characteristics of

Mesoamerica which we will discuss further were already established.

Next in our timeline is the classic period, from around 150 to 300 up until 650 to 900, followed by the postclassic period, from the end of the classic era to about 1519. The postclassic period may be divided into early postclassic—900 to 1250 approximately—and late postclassic—1250 to 1519.

During these periods, Mesoamerican cultures grew and flourished. They interacted and highly influenced each other, all while adapting to the changes with which they were faced along the way.

Similarities and Differences Between Different Mesoamerican Cultures

As we established at the beginning of this chapter, Mesoamerica is a cultural region. This means that, while different groups of people coexisted in Mesoamerica throughout its history, they had their fair share of similarities. For this reason, there are topics that might continually come up throughout this book, because they will be common to various, or even all, the Mesoamerican civilization discussed here.

The architecture of the cities, for example,

has a common pattern due to the heavy impact that religion and rituals had within it—religion and rituals were fairly common throughout Mesoamerica, despite there being differences between one culture and the next, such as the names of specific gods. Ceremonies such as the ball game were also not exclusive to only one particular civilization. Nor was the 260-day calendar, or even the construction of pyramids.

Even the Incas, being an Andean culture and not strictly Mesoamerican by the very definition we have given to the term in this chapter, do present similarities with the rest of the cultures studied in this book.

Of course, there are also traits that separate these cultures from one another and one of these traits is language. We must consider that Mesoamerica has some 140 different languages, divided into various families plus some insulated languages. This becomes relevant for the reader of this book, insofar as some native words in some of those languages are used to refer to some key concepts. In order to keep this book and its content as simple and easy to understand as possible, whenever a certain term in the native language of a particular culture is used, a translation is provided. If it's necessary, a more in-depth explanation is given. For further study about the languages of the fascinating world that is Mesoamerica, the reader may turn to works such as Comparative Linguistics of Mesoamerican Languages Today, by Lyle Campbell.

Having thus determined the time and space that this book is going to cover, and having also established the massive cultural shock that was produced upon the arrival of the Europeans, we may now start our journey through the different Mesoamerican civilizations.

CHAPTER 2
THE OLMEC CIVILIZATION — THE FIRST GREAT CIVILIZATION OF MESOAMERICA

Defining "Olmec"

The Olmecs, who were located in the modern states of Tabasco and Veracruz in the southern-central region of Mexico, are the first human group in Mesoamerica we can identify as a civilization. They inhabited tropical lowlands and we can consider them the civilization from which the Mayans arose. Their main area, what we can call the Metropolitan Olmec area, was around 6,000 to 7,000 square miles, or a little over 15,500 to 18,000 square kilometers, in extension. Their limits were given mostly by their natural geographical surroundings: the Gulf of Mexico serves as the northern border, the mountains provide the southern one. To the east and west were rivers, the Blasillo-Tonalá and the Papaloapan respectively.

The very word we use, "Olmec", can have more than one clear meaning. The Aztecs, for example, used it to denote the inhabitants of the Gulf of Mexico—specifically the inhabitants of the southern coast of said Gulf—during a specific time period, between approximately 1400 and 1600. But as the reader will note, the Aztec definition of the Olmecs is not compatible with the one given just above. At least, not unless the Olmecs identified by the Aztecs in the 15th and 16th centuries match the ones identified as the first civilization to exist in that geographical region. Evidently, the timeline for the Aztec definition is way later than the first definition. Unfortunately, they don't coincide. The Olmecs that the Aztecs talked about were not the same Olmecs that inhabited the region a couple of millennia before.

These are not the only two definitions of the word "Olmec" that we can find. The same word is used—in modern times—to indicate a certain art style which was produced mainly in the area identified with the Olmecs: the lowlands of the southern Gulf of Mexico. Another definition used today identifies the Olmecs as an archaeological culture i.e. a culture recognized by a distinctive type of object repeatedly found in a specific geographical area that lived between approximately 1,500 to 400 B.C.E. in the southern Gulf Coast area. This one seems to coincide with the first definition given, but adding the important fact that Olmecs had a very distinct type of art, as the definition suggested just before pointed out; let this important detail be added to the definition of the culture then. As for the Aztecs, their definition clearly referred to some other culture living in that area in their times.

This does not, in any possible way, close the debate about what actually defines Olmec culture. Just as many things said in this book may refer to a certain position in a debate that will perhaps never be truly closed. Knowledge is always growing and changing, and the temporal distance between us and the civilization one studies makes it even more difficult to really find the one and definitive right answer. But as happens with so many topics when studying history, the debate will be closed here for the sake of moving on.

Olmec Stone Art: Serpentine and Jade

Being, as it is, important to the very definition of the word "Olmec", it is necessary to devote some words to the subject of Olmec art.

One of its distinctive traits was its frequent

use of stone, specifically serpentine and jade, to produce carved objects. The main difference between them is that serpentine is not as hard of a stone as jade. Barring that distinction, they were treated equally, with both serving as symbols of wealth and being associated with maize, a symbol of fertility among the Olmecs. Jade was also associated with the very breath or spirit of life. It is very possible that the Olmecs participated in the custom—which was shared by various peoples in prehispanic Mesoamerica—of burying the dead with a bead of jade in their mouth, as a body buried in Oaxaca seems to indicate.

To produce the stone figure, a rough sketch of it was first cut out of the piece of stone, and then it was ground and polished. Further than those basic steps, the stone could be worked on by sawing it, using a kind of saw also made of stone which was moved back and forth, or by drilling it using a form of drill. This last technique could be useful when it was time to, for example, work on the earlobes of a statue. They could be perforated by drilling them, to allow jewelry to be worn by the statue—although this was not very common. On other occasions, drilling was used to perforate the nasal septum of the statue—the division between the two nostrils. This was perhaps done to allow another piece of jewelry to be added to the statue, or perhaps to ritually infuse the breath of life into it. Another feature various Olmec figures have is the inclusion of beads, or similar elements right in front of the nose of the figure, which is also shared by Maya sculptures.

Inhabitants of the Jungle: Making the Best of One's Circumstances
Agriculture in a Tropical Climate

The Olmecs lived in an area dominated by jungle on the one hand, and rich in water sources, on the other. Because of this, they were fortunate enough to have at their disposal a considerable source of aquatic food, such as fish and shellfish, which were not available to inhabitants of other areas, because the Olmec territory had an abundance of rivers and lagoons, as well as the sea which was their natural border to the north. This was beneficial, as they had access to nutrients that others didn't.

But the situation also posed its challenges, namely in dealing with agriculture. The Olmecs still needed agriculture to get by, much like the rest of the Mesoamerican cultures. They used the same basic products, such as beans, corn, and squash that the other inhabitants of the Mesoamerican region also used. They further needed to resort to agricultural methods that helped them solve the problem of the jungle covering most of the terrain. Of course, commerce was a great way for the Olmecs to gain access to products they couldn't produce themselves, and the rivers could prove very useful in this regard. They could provide communication and thus, facilitate commerce. But they also needed to be able to cultivate their own crops, probably by periodic flooding. This theory lines up with the geography of many Olmec sites, which are actually islands. The water around those islands periodically falls and rises, which could be used to help agriculture.

Olmec Demography and Political Organization

Given that the Olmecs expanded rather extensively outside of their primary area, we could say that their population was large—too large, in fact, to be adequately sustained in an area the size of the one they had primarily inhabited. Archeological findings provide a clue as to a possible explanation for the Olmecs' expansion and that explanation may lie in the pressure of having to sustain an ever growing population. In the words of Bernal (1969): "If we judge by cultural remains, toward the beginning of the first millenium B.C. no other area of Mesoamerica was so densely populated. Thus it is that the centrifugal movement of the Olmecs becomes comprehensible."

It might be tempting to think the difficulties deriving from the tropical climate, stated above, would render the area very difficult for a human group to thrive in; but the situation was not exactly the way we might think of it today.

For example, diseases caused by contaminated water, which were a huge problem in the 16th century and forward, were not such a big problem for the Olmecs. The reason for this was simple: the Olmecs didn't have domestic animals. This was a disadvantage in some ways, such as for transportation, but an advantage when it came to the cleanliness of the water, due to the fact that there weren't any animals using the same water the people used. Malaria is another prominent cause of disease and death in climates such as the one the Olmecs experienced daily, but it might have been introduced to the region after the Olmec period and thus not have been such a problem. The Olmecs seem to have avoided two of the largest problems a present-day inhabitant of their region has to face.

As for the political organization of the Olmecs, this has proven to be rather hard to determine precisely. Some view the Olmecs as being more or less equivalent with their contemporaries in terms of their sociopolitical organization—which means that all cultures could influence each other in more or less equal terms—while others state that they were actually at a decidedly superior level. This would mean that the influence was much more unilateral from the Olmecs to the rest of the surrounding people. Those who favor the second position may even go as far as to say that the Olmecs were a sort of Mesoamerican "mother culture", acting as the point of origin for the rest of the civilizations that lived in the area.

La Venta and San Lorenzo: the Main Olmec Sites

La Venta

One of the main Olmec sites is a civic and ceremonial center known as La Venta, located in the western part of the state of Tabasco. Specifically, it's located in the coastal region, around ten to a dozen miles inland in an area populated by streams and sloughs which drain in the Río Tomalá—the Tomalá River. It's surrounded by difficult terrain, since the region we're describing is a very swampy one. The site itself is an island, around 3,7 to 4,4 miles.

Several archaeological remains can be found in La Venta. The biggest mound in the site—the Great Mound—is the most prominent landmark. It rises a little over 105 feet above the ground surrounding it, which includes a platform on which it rests. This platform has more or less a square shape, with each side measuring nearly 394 feet. A bit to the north—some 328 feet—there is a group composed of a rectangular ceremonial court, complete with basalt columns to enclose it, and three other mounds, considerably smaller than the great mound (the tallest one being around 13 feet high).

There are two archaeologically interesting findings to be made as one looks to the south of the Great Mound. First, there is a giant head made of stone, with a stela not far from it. A stela is an upright piece of stone, typically in the form of a column or a slab. Stelae can serve to identify gravestones, and they can carry inscriptions.

Secondly, another group of archaeological remains can be found. In this group we can identify several mounds, one elongated, one rather pyramidal in size, and some others in the southern part of the group. The elongated mound has a stone altar to each side of it and several columns.

These remains depict the importance that religious life had for the Olmecs, just as it did for all Mesoamerican people: the altars and the ceremonial court that still remain in our present day are a testimony of that.

Another prominent motif found in La Venta is that of maize. The Olmecs depicted maize in three distinct ways. The first is the tripartite maize, that is, a cob represented with a leaf on each side of it, each of these elements being separate from the others. The second form is banded maize; and the third and final form is maize depicted with flowing silk, a flowing element protruding from the cob. If the reader should want to take a look at pictures of these representations of maize, as well as other forms of Olmec art, he or she is welcome to consult the book Olmec Art at Dumbarton Oaks, by Karl A. Taube.

Maize representation, just as it did for other cultures, held for the Olmecs a great religious meaning. Olmecs believed in no small amount of supernatural creatures and these were, of course, depicted in various items of art, just as the grand theme of fertility and the cosmos also made its way into artistic expression.

Beyond their artistic representation, it is important to mention how vital the Olmec religion was to the whole of Mesoamerica. As an example of this, many gods venerated by other cultures in the region and associated with the natural powers of rain and lightning, such as the Mayan god Chaak, seem to derive from an Olmec deity. This is in full accordance with the position of the Olmecs as the most ancient of Mesoamerican civilizations; naturally, being the first to inhabit the region, it's easy for them to have a high impact on the cultures that come after them as they come in contact with each other.

San Lorenzo

Along with La Venta, San Lorenzo is among the most important Olmec sites. It is located in the state of Veracruz, specifically in the municipality of Texistepec. The landscape surrounding the site is rich in water, as it is located in the drainage of the river Río Coatzacoalcos. Just as with La Venta, San Lorenzo was strategically placed upon high ground, in a location where the river allowed for easy communication and trade. Transportation was also facilitated by the location of the site. Even in the dry season, the drivers were there to provide the necessary routes and in the rainy months there were even more options, because of the channels that filled up with water.

In the site, a considerable number of monuments can be found. Some of them are giant heads sculpted in stone, perhaps depicting past Olmec rulers, or other high-profile individuals. This can be deduced from the way the heads are carved, with a careful style that makes the face look quite lifelike. It bears mentioning also, that the great pieces of rock that these sculptures were made out of were not easily moved. The cost and logistics of their transportation seem to indicate a highly hierarchical society.

Archaeologists were also able to find altars of which many of the figures that the Olmecs produced were human, or at least anthropomorphic, with some animals also being commonly represented such as jaguars, eagles, stingrays, and snakes.

The jaguar was probably used to symbolize supernatural creatures. It was considered the most important animal in Mesoamerica when it came to representations of power; thus, a jaguar-like characteristic, such as a great snarl, marked the being so represented as a powerful and other-wordly one. The Olmec figures that most prominently show this duality between an anthropologic being and the mighty jaguar, are the ones that literally represent the moment when a shaman, entering a state of ecstatic trance, turns into a jaguar, at least according to Furst (1998), as cited by Taube (2004). These are called transformation figures.

Most of the sculptures can be found in the central region of the site, which is also where the ruler lived, along with his family and, in general, the entirety of the elite. An important finding done in this area, the so-called "Red Palace", gives us a notion of this by its use of stone. This type of material was expensive and therefore serves as a symbol of status. The commoners had their houses on the sides of the site, made with much more humble materials such as mud for the walls and palm thatch for the roofs.

CHAPTER 3
THE ZAPOTEC CIVILIZATION — MONTE ALBAN AND MITLA

The Zapotecs: Evolution and Society
The Four Steps of Zapotec Evolution

The Zapotecs inhabited southern Mexico, originating from the Valley of Oaxaca. Just like the Olmecs, they were also among the first civilizations to inhabit Mesoamerica. The Zapotecs also had to contend with less than ideal conditions for agriculture. Anne Kirkby (1974), as cited by Flannery and Marcus (1976), summed up the situation by saying that, in that particular region, there were actually more years in which the harvest failed than years in which it was an actual success. The explanation of their success includes more than one singular reason, but factors such as the use of an irrigation system so as not to depend too heavily only on natural rains and trade as a means to get access to products the Zapotecs couldn't grow themselves, may be counted among the reasons. In the end, they thrived for 3,000 years and that's the most important point after all.

As often happens with Mesoamerican people, the history of the Zapotecs may be divided into different stages. In this case, there are four stages that can be distinguished one from another, making up between them the prehistory of the Valley of Oaxaca.

The first stage was a very primitive one: semi nomadic hunter-gatherers populated the area in the beginning and began incorporating agriculture into their lives. Once agriculture was well established, agricultural villages began to appear, marking the transition to a fully sedentary lifestyle. This period lasted from about 1,500 to 500 B.C.E. and reached a much higher population density than the first one, due to the benefits brought about by agriculture.

Many of the traits associated with the Zapotecs originated during this period and certainly agriculture was not the least of them. Zapotecs were very good farmers and their techniques showed it. They differentiated between irrigable fields—called queéla huiza—and non-irrigable ones—or quéela pichijta. They used irrigation and were able to work with both surface water sources and subterranean ones;

they even studied the rainfall just before the rainy season and adjusted their actions accordingly. They did not, though, seek to necessarily exploit the land to its maximum capacity and obtain from it as much product as they could have: they rather preferred to limit themselves to obtain what they and their families needed to survive and to fulfill their religious obligations. This can be explained because Zapotecs believed that both bad and good things—such as good and bad luck—had to be in harmony with each other. Good things, they believed, were not infinite, and one must not take more of it than necessary, lest someone else may not not get their share.

The transition to the next phase of Zapotec development was produced by the foundation of Monte Albán, which is mentioned in some more detail later on in this very chapter. For now, suffice it to say that, for a thousand years the Zapotecs would base their civilization around Monte Albán. In a similar fashion, the fourth and final stage was brought about by the decline of the same city of Monte Albán around 700, which opened a long period of military tensions in the region which lasted until the Spanish conquest of the territory in 1521.

What the Spaniards Found: Zapotec Society

When the Spaniards came into contact with the Zapotecs within the fourth and last stage of their evolution, they found a highly hierarchical society. There were three clearly distinguishable social classes: the commoners, the nobility, and the priesthood. The nobles had the task of overseeing the communities inhabited by the commoners: a member of this group, called a coqui, was assigned to each community. The nobility was also the source from when the priesthood emerged, because the priests were chosen from these ranks. Above everybody else, of course, was the great lord or coquitao, the Zapotec equivalent to a king.

As for the resources needed to sustain the Zapotec people, each community had to pay its share to the lord's collector, or golaba, as in modern times when we must pay taxes that the state then uses to the benefit of the community. The Zapotecs were also able to conquer towns belonging to different people, and these towns had to then also pay tribute.

Zapotec Religion
Pée (Pi), the Vital Force

For the Zapotecs, things could be divided— very broadly—into two great categories: those that were actual living things and those who weren't. They used the word pée, or pi, to designate the vital force which was the difference between the two categories. One is somehow reminded of the Bible, specifically of Genesis 2:7 (NIV), where God, having created man, proceeds to give him "the breath of life." In the words of the Bible: "Then the Lord God formed a man from the dust of the ground and breathed into his nostrils the breath of life, and the man became a living being." (Bible Gateway, s.f.)

The difference here is that, for the Zapotecs, pée was present in many more creatures than just human beings, even in what we now know as inanimate objects. Basically, having movement was indicative of having pée. Whatever didn't have pée—what the Zapotecs considered to be inanimate objects, considering "having vital force" as equivalent to "being animated" and vice versa—could be manipulated in whichever way humans chose to, by whichever ingenuity, skill or technology.

Anything that could move and therefore had pée, the sacred "spirit" (also possible to translate as "wind" or "breath"), was considered sacred, thus had to be treated with respect. There was no possibility to manipulate these living elements, as one could manipulate the non-living things. Instead, one had to create a relationship with them and address them in appropriate rituals to, for example, make requests. This, of course, included presenting whichever Great Spirit did actually grant a request with the adequate offerings, be it food, blood, incense, a sacrificed being (either animal or even human), among other possibilities.

Lightning was a living thing for the Zapotecs and they could be asked respectfully to pierce the clouds by addressing them as "Great Spirit Within Lightning", or Pitáo Cociyo. By piercing the clouds and letting the rain down, "Lightning" allowed the Zapotecs to use the water obtained from rain, which—as a living thing—could not be utilized otherwise. "Earthquake" was another powerful force, which could be asked to stop punishing "Earth". It was addressed as "Great Spirit Within the Earthquake", or Pitáo Xóo. The other great universal forces, the most powerful in the Zapotec world, were the clouds, hail, wind, and fire.

The "Old People in the Clouds" and Communication With the Spirit World

The Zapotecs believed firmly in the possibility of humans transforming after death to become some other form of life. They also used different narcotic substances—from tobacco to hallucinogenic mushrooms—to communicate with the spirit world such as with their ancestors. These ancestors were believed to have transformed into the clouds, thus being referred to as the "old people in the clouds", or penigólazaa. They could be reached by smoke elevating up to the clouds, be it from incense (yála) or from burning a human heart in charcoal. Communication with the pinigólazaa was to be approached carefully if one desired a positive outcome: something must be offered before a request was made, as well as when it was granted. This was important because without those offerings, the pinigólazaa could not adequately intercede with supernatural spirits on behalf of the descendants who needed it. There was a wide variety of possible offerings from food, drink, or blood to a sacrificed living creature who could, in turn, range from an animal such as a turkey, to a child, to a fully grown adult. One of the best animals for sacrifice, in the eyes of the Zapotecs, was the quail, viewed as "pure" or "clean" due to its preference for clean water—like dew drops— instead of dirty water.

The Zapotec Ritual Calendar
The Zapotec ritual calendar was another "living thing", something that had the vital force of pée. This is even suggested in the name by

which the Zapotecs called this calendar: piye.

The piye ran parallel to the secular 365-day calendar. It had a duration of 260 days, divided in four 65 day "lightings", or cociyos, each also referred to as pitáo, or "great spirit". Its importance was great, because many Zapotec rituals were scheduled in accordance with it.

The ritual calendar was not exclusive to the Zapotecs, but rather a common trait between Mesoamerican cultures.

Temples and Priests

There were clear ranks among the Zapotec priesthood. At the top of it were the uija-táo, or high priests, greatly respected because of their power to predict the future and interact closely with the great spirits. It was them who consulted the spirits directly, with the results of these consultations then being passed on down the chain of command. Their advice was taken very seriously by the ruler. The copa pitáo, regular or ordinary priests, also derived from the upper social classes. Below the copa pitáo were the colanij, the diviners. They had the task of helping individual, regular people in their everyday lives by helping them make important decisions about subjects such as marriage and children. Of course, it wasn't the colanij who made the decision for the individual seeking advice: rather, it was fate through the colanij. There were also other religious people with minor roles.

As for the temples, a typical Zapotec temple reflected in its architecture a separation between the priests, on one hand, and the common folk, on the other. The temple consisted of two rooms: the sacred, inner one where the priest would perform the actual sacrifice, and the outer room, where the person wishing to offer said sacrifice could enter in order to request a sacrifice. Only priests could enter the inner room.

These temples were referred to as "house of the vital force", or "sacred house", yoho pée.

Blood Sacrifices
As mentioned above, Zapotecs did not only offer sacrifices of things like food and other objects; or sacrifices where they killed a person—for example a slave or a war captive. They also offered blood sacrifices in the form of a literal offering of blood. Unlike the animal or human sacrifices, which were left to the priest, the blood sacrifices could be, and were, performed by the citizens themselves. The person simply used an adequate object—such as a shark's tooth, among other options—to let out just a little bit of blood and then collected it on a

feather, a bit of grass, or other material for the offering.

Monte Albán

Monte Albán was the Zapotec capital for more than a millennium. It was founded around 500 B.C.E. in the valley of Oaxaca, Mexico, and it continued to be the capital of the Zapotecs until around 800. Its population reached about 25,000 thousand people, making it the greatest city of its region in the highlands of southern Mexico.

At the center of urban Monte Albán we find a Main Plaza, some 985 feet in length. The urban center in its totality was about 25 m2 (square miles).

In this regard, Monte Albán was far bigger than the villages that the Zapotecs inhabited before it was founded. These little agricultural villages had around 100 inhabitants each, or around five to twenty families. The foundation of such a big urban center as Monte Albán was a result of the population growth over time and the subsequent change in dynamics between the different inhabitants of the region. In addition to its size and population, Monte Alban also brought about another change: it housed, not only related families as the earlier villages did, but also non-related ones, which possibly wouldn't have come into contact with each other in other circumstances.

In the early history of Monte Alban, burial traditions dictated that most adults be buried near their house of residence. They were accompanied in their graves by personal artifacts and some offerings. The burial practices for children, on the other hand, have remained a mystery.

Tombs made a somewhat later appearance. In general the bigger the tomb, the bigger the house it's associated with, and the more numerous and sophisticated the offerings in the tomb. The big change that the use of tombs produced was incorporating a piece of architecture designed for multiple uses and not only one as would be the case with a grave. This can represent an archaeological difficulty, because tombs were often opened and reused, and that history is sometimes confusing for an archaeologist working with mortuary remains.

Mitla

Mitla is another great Zapotec site in the state of Oaxaca, being second in importance only to Monte Albán. It was one of the focal points of Zapotec power in the region, extending its influence through the Eastern Oaxaca Valley and the Sierra Madre.

The Zapotecs called the place liobaa, which translates as "house of tombs", while the nahuatl word for it was mictlan, which can be translated as "valley of the dead", or "place of the dead". Its peak occurred around 1000 to 1521, and during its prime it came to be a fairly prosperous place, with great buildings and an estimated population of around 10,500 inhabitants.

The site is even open to the public today, offering tourists the possibility to roam around what were probably the public buildings of the city. Many archeological remains can be found in Mitla, divided into five groups. Different remains can be found in each group, and according to Mitla, Oaxaca (2016) interesting facts have been found about each of them.

One of the groups, possibly the one with the second oldest building of the five, contains remains that are all made of adobe; that's why the group is called "el grupo de los adobes", or "the adobe group". It contains four mounds surrounding a central square, and a plaza. Three of the four mounds are relatively short, and unimportant, but the fourth one, the eastern one, is bigger and more prominent, making it in all likelihood a former temple, or palace. Another group, referred to as "el grupo del sur" or "the southern group", contains the same basic buildings, distributed the same way. It is believed that the remains in the "grupo del sur" are older than the one in the "grupo de los adobes", making them the oldest remains in Mitla.

Another group is "el grupo de la Iglesia" or "the church group", which derives its name from the church that was built there. In this group we can find three quadrangles, all looking north to south, all in different sizes, and at different levels.

The so-called "grupo de las columnas", or "the column group", has a similar set of remains distributed in a similar way, but it contains six beautiful monolithic columns, which can be exclusively found in Mitla and which give this group its name. They are in a room adjacent to one of the quadrangles, which is a beautiful and richly decorated palace. There were also tombs found in one of the quadrangles of this group.

Finally, the fifth and last group, the "grupo del arroyo" or "group of the stream"—possibly named in honor of a nearby water source—is pretty similar to the other two.

CHAPTER 4
THE TEOTIHUACAN CIVILIZATION — A MONUMENTAL CITY OF THE ANCIENT WORLD

The Teotihuacán culture is known today through its most prominent city, its namesake Teotihuacán. The city lends the culture its name. Sadly, no other cities belonging to this culture have left remnants that we can study today, which leaves the city of Teotihuacán as our main source of information about the civilization of the same name.

The history of the great city of Teotihuacán is rather a long one, starting around the year 50 and ending around 650. This 700year period has been divided into smaller segments. These segments are:

- Tazcuali period, dating from 50 to 150
- Miccaotili period, dating from 150 to 225

- Early Tlanimilolpa period, dating from 225 to 300
- Late Tlanimilolpa period, dating from 300 to 350
- Early Xolalpan period, dating from 350 to 450
- Late Xolalpan period, dating from 450 to 550
- Metepec period, dating from 550 to 650

This division is in accordance with Braswell 2003b and Cowgill 1997, 2003b (Headrick, 2007).

This city was located in the Valley of Mexico, nearly 48.5 miles away from present-day Mexico City. It was a big and prosperous city, well respected within the region, and the basis for its sustenance was agriculture and commerce, similarly to other Mesoamerican cultures.

Teotihuacán, the Sacred City of the Valley of Mexico

The population of Toetihuacán was the bulk of the actual population of the Valley of Mexico. In fact, it was a policy of the Teotihuacanos to try and keep the population rather concentrated in that area. That way, they had control over most of the population of the Valley of Mexico, of which the Valley of Teotihuacán is only a portion located in the north-eastern area of the greater valley. As a result of this, part of the Valley of Mexico stayed semi-abandoned, not being utilized to its full potential the way it had been before Teotihuacán. But, the Teotihuacanos valued political control over the full use of the resources of the Valley, and this kind of attitude might help us understand why Teotihuacán grew to be such an important city in its time.

In addition to its political greatness, Teotihuacán was, above all, the most prominent religious center of its time. It was home to multiple temples, magnificent pyramids— such as the Pyramid of the Sun and of the Moon—and the awe-inspiring Avenue of the Dead. Nothing was done on a subdued scale! It is very possible that the Teotihuacanos even considered their city as sacred. Throughout its history, the political, and the religious aspects of life seemed to be quite tightly related for the inhabitants of the city even merged into one.

What Kind of City Was Teotihuacán?

Teotihuacán was attractive to people because it was a prosperous city, with excellent commercial standing in spite of not having a port, and thus offered good opportunities for a successful, pleasant life, if one was okay with the fact of having to work with no beasts of burden to help. Of course, its dense population and the fact that it was built rather early, meant that some diseases did pose a threat; but this was no different from other cities with similar characteristics.

It was also a great political and religious capital, but without the strong dynastic element of other similar cities. It is believed that it became successful thanks to the work and guidance of powerful rulers who reigned during the first part of the history of the great city. This seems to be confirmed by the existence of such magnificent temples, as the pyramids of the Moon, Sun, and Feathered Serpent, which as archaeologists believe, were constructed to commemorate said strong rulers. But after that, things started to change.

Once the main architectural focus shifted from public buildings to private housing, which happened around the year 200, very few great pyramids were built thereafter to go alongside the existing ones. That meant that much less time and energy were invested in personally glorifying a specific person, such as a ruler.

There is also the fact that, unlike Maya kings who loved to tell the stories of their glorious deeds in pieces of art such as stela, the

Teotihuacanos did not write such detailed narratives. In addition to that, as the reader may perhaps appreciate after having read about the Avenue of the Dead, the focus of attention was not on the palaces, but rather on the architecture of the referred main street of the city, leaving the palaces in a considerably lower scale to those of, for example, Mayan kings. What some experts may have one day considered to be palaces, may simply be the residence of some elite citizens and not, necessarily, that of the ruler.

Details like these make some experts believe that Teotihuacán may have turned to a more collective form of ruling, in which no individual held such a prominent position as the rulers of other peoples did. This might have helped to keep the peace in a city that had a multi-ethnic population which, of course, would find a more collective discourse easier to agree on. In matters of religion, unity was incentivized by bringing attention to the common interests shared by all the population, such as having enough rain, and enjoying agricultural prosperity, keeping the cosmic order in balance by keeping the gods satisfied, and keeping the city economically and militarily thriving.

The latter was important because the city did

not even have proper fortification. This would have left the city vulnerable to attacks and, in fact, the periphery of the city was a relatively easy target. But, in general, the city was simply big enough that it needed not to fear any particular threat. The sheer size of the whole city, along with its architecture—which included walls in certain places—protected this great city. It also helped to have a very organized army.

All of these characteristics made Teotihuacán a remarkable city, successful to an incredible degree, all while doing things much in the way of the Teotihuacanos, different from the way others would.

The city would eventually decline and collapse in the sixth century, perhaps due to environmental reasons, or to migrations, or to political reasons; it is still not perfectly clear which causes are the true ones. But, even then, in the midst of its collapse, Teotihuacán did not completely lose its power straight away. One to two hundred years after its collapse, it also retained a considerable population count. It did undergo a major transformation when it collapsed, it did so precisely because of its former glory. A lesser city, devoid of any great importance, could perhaps last longer with little to no great alterations to the way it functions;

but, the higher the city—or the civilization—goes, the worse the subsequent fall will inevitably be.

The Visual Wonder of Teotihuacán: the Avenue of the Dead

The main street of Teotihuacán was the Avenue of the Dead, which was once three miles long. This road ran through the north-south axis and was supposed to be traversed from south to north. If one did so, one was walking directly toward the impressive volcano known as Cerro Gordo and, naturally, couldn't help but marvel at it. The positioning of this avenue is a clear indication of the efforts the Teotihuacanos made to use their natural surroundings to their advantage when designing their city.

As one walked northwards along the Avenue of the Dead, one also moved progressively upwards, as one progressed from the lower southern part of the city to the higher northern one. The final destination was the Pyramid of the Moon, one of Teotihuacán's main temples, which integrated beautifully with the volcano. The other great pyramid of the city, even larger that the Pyramid of the Moon, was the Pyramid of the Sun, somehow eclipsed by the former's positioning. The third important pyramid found within the city was the Pyramid of the Feathered

Serpent.

The Avenue of the Dead served as the focal point of daily life in Teotihuacán, hosting a myriad of social, political and religious activities.

Housing in Teotihuacán: Apartment Compounds and Barrios

During the period spanning from around the year 200 to 350, the Teotihuacanos focused their energy on building domestic units capable of housing their sizable population, after a period of centering their attention on the pyramids representing the public, religious side of life.

Around 2,000 apartment compounds were built. Each compound was square or rectangular in shape, and contained a series of patios, each surrounded by rooms. The roof of the patios, which was pierced to let air in, was the only source of ventilation, because there were no windows on the compound. One of these patios—the ritual patio—often had a small altar, which could be used for rituals. The patios were also the place for daily activities, being more agreeable than the more enclosed indoor spaces of the compounds. A series of narrow little streets separated one compound from another.

Teotihuacán was also divided into neighborhoods, or barrios as it's said in Spanish. Normally, a barrio would consist of a group of people with a specific trait in common. This trait could be a common craft, or profession to use modern terms: for example a barrio of potters; or a certain social position, like in a barrio found in 1983 which is believed to have been the home to relatively upper-class people, or a barrio inhabited by foreigners.

Activities in Teotihuacán

In addition to the agricultural activities necessary to sustain its population, the Teotihuacanos engaged in various forms of craft. These crafts included pottery, lapidary work, and several lines of work aimed at helping in the construction of the magnificent buildings of the city, from those who made the concrete used in floors and ceilings to those who cut the stones needed in the construction.

The most widely used material when it came to piercing and cutting was obsidian. One example of its use was for weapons, such as projectile points found in great burial pits containing the corpses of many sacrificed people. These projectile points, along with other offerings, are a testimony of the importance of military affairs in the eyes of the Teotihuacanos, for the offerings had a military significance. While there is no evidence that the state exercised an actual direct control over the production of obsidian objects and their exchange, the subject was not devoid of interest to the state, which reflects a probably important role played by this material in the economical and everyday life of the city.

The Gods of Teotihuacán
The God of Rain

The most important of the Teotihuacan gods was the god of rain. He was depicted in many objects of art. The god of rain was similar to deities found in pieces of art originating from La Venta, and he is also similar to his Aztec counterpart, Tláloc.

The representations of the rain god found in Teotihuacán combine characteristics from two animals, with a great deal of significance in the eyes of the Measoamerican: the jaguar and the serpent. He shows his affinity with the powerful jaguar through his long fangs, or through his right hand, which is transformed into a jaguar claw or—alternatively—holds a mitten resembling one. He equally shows his affinity with the fierce serpent by being depicted with a bifid tongue resembling that of the reptile, or by being depicted alongside servants who are wearing helmets decorated with snakes, as is found in a depiction of red Tlalocs—yes, plural—originating in Tepantitla. The Tepantitla Tlalocs are also depicted within a frame consisting of decorated snakes.

Some depictions of the god of rain may also be shown with elements symbolic of other animals, such as the quetzal—a type of bird—the owl, and the butterfly.

Other Depictions of Deities

The god of fire is also depicted in Teotihuacán art, being the second most distinguishable Teotihuacán god—judging by artistic representation—after the god of rain. The image of the god of fire is described as the following "De ellos, el mejor definido, después del de la lluvia, es el del fuego, representado en esculturas de piedra como un viejo desnudo que sostiene en la cabeza un brasero o incensario (...) correspondiente al anecúyotl, la mitra del dios del fuego (Xiuhtecuhtli Hueheteotl) de los mexicanos." (Armillas, 1945).

Translating into English as "Of them [the gods], the best defined one, after that of rain, is that of fire, depicted in stone sculptures as a naked old man holding in his head a brazier or censer (...) corresponding to the anécuyotl, the miter of the Mexican fire god (Xiuhtecuhtli Hueheteotl)."

An image of a masked individual, commonly found in Teotihuacán art, is believed by some, like the German anthropologist Eduard Seller, to be depictions of the god of vegetal renewal, Xipe Totec; but,this is not definitive.

Another artistic representation also common in Teotihuacán, that of the head of a bald man, is also believed to be the depiction of a god, although his characteristics and identity are not clear. This kind of representation is found beyond Teotihuacán.

The image of this bald man is quite interesting and peculiar. In the words of archeologist, Pedros Armillas (1945) "Lleva siempre un peinado especial con la frente rapada y a veces le cae sobre ella un flequillo de pelo corto, un mechón o algo que parece un copo de algodón; otras luce dos anillos colocados también sobre la frente o un tocado formado por tres penachos de pluma, dispuestos figurando las alas y la cola de un ave."

Translating into English as "He's always wearing a special hairstyle, shaven in the forehead, and sometimes he's got a frill of short hair falling on it [his forehead], or a lock or something that looks like a cotton ball; other times he's wearing two earrings, also placed upon his forehead, or a headdress made of three plumes of feathers, arranged in the shape of the wings and tail of a bird."

The Case of the Facade of the Temple of Quetzalcoatl

The facade of the Temple of Quetzalcoátl, located in Teotihuacán, is certainly remarkable among Teotihuacán pieces of art. It presents an interesting dilemma concerning the feathered serpents represented there, and the name of the temple itself. Did the Teotihuacanos actually know such a deity as Quetzalcoátl? It certainly is easy to give the temple the name of said deity, because Teotihuacán was commonly associated with Tula, the city of Quetzalcoátl precisely around the time that the temple was discovered; but, this does not automatically mean that the actual Teotihuacanos had Quetzalcoatl among their own gods.

It seems, in fact, rather dubious that the feathered serpents of the temple are an actual depiction of Quetzalcoátl, because there are no other depictions of him in Teotihuacán culture. Besides, there is already a major god—the god of rain, the Teotihuacán version of Tláloc—associated with the serpent. Moreover, the depictions found in the temple are practically identical to the ones associated with the Palacio de Tepantitla, which is known to be devoted to the god of rain, So it's reasonable to think that the god of rain is the one that the temple was dedicated to.

It's actually highly likely that the god of rain acts as a sort of replacement or equivalent to Quetzalcóatl in Teotihuacán culture. To further quote Armillas (1945) "Ahora bien, aunque Quetzalcoatl no aparezca individualizado en Teotihuacán, es posible que alguno de los conceptos que con él se relacionan haya existido allí, pero no aisladamente, sino incluído en la idea de Tlaloc."

The latter translates into English as "Now, although Quetzalcoatl may not appear individualized in Tenochtitlán, it is still possible that the concepts associated with him have existed there, just not in isolation, but rather included in the idea of Tláloc."

This should come as no surprise at all, for it is perfectly coherent with the high degree of similitude exhibited by different Mesoamerican pantheons. The close bond between the Mesoamerican gods and concepts such as the forces of nature, implied in the quote from Armillas, may be the explanation for this, in the sense that Mesoamerican gods can be viewed as representations of those concepts, and each specific culture chooses its particular way of representing each of those concepts. The case of the facade of the temple of Quetzalcoátl is representative of a problem that whoever decides to pursue archaeological endeavors will always face, and which was alluded to at the very beginning of this book: the fact that we always learn about other cultures and other times starting from our own biases, reality, and experiences. It was easy to simply name the temple in honor of Quetzalcoátl because of the association of Teotihuacán with another city, but that association was made by the experts who discovered the ruins of the temple, not necessarily by the builders of the temple themselves.

CHAPTER 5

THE MAYA — THE GREAT ASTRONOMERS OF MESOAMERICA

From Nomads to Creators of Great Cities: Periods of Mayan History

Mayans had a rather important difference with the Olmecs that they derived from. They were organized in various groups—scattered through several states of present-day Mexico, Belize, El Salvador, Guatemala, and the west portion of Honduras—rather than being all under one centralized power. Of course, these groups had enough in common to be considered as part of a cultural unity; but, there are specific traits as well.

Geographically speaking, a distinction may be made between the Mayans inhabiting the Highlands and the Lowlands, and between the Mayans of the northern, central, and southern areas; but, we can also distinguish, from a chronological perspective, a pre-classic period from a classic one, and a post classic one.

The pre-classic period can be defined as starting around the year 1,800 B.C.E. and ending around the year 250. Mayans started as nomad groups, in Cuelo (Belize), around 2000 B.C.E. Around two hundred years later, they started to become sedentary and the first settlements started to appear in the state of Chiapas, in Mexico. With time, their little villages started to grow and gave rise to bigger urban centers. One such urban center was the city of El Mirador, built in northern Guatemala. It had a big central square, a large central pyramid and other buildings. Its story spans over several centuries (200 B.C.E to 150). Another big city certainly worth mentioning is Teotihuacán, which influenced other cities such as Monte Albán and Tikal (Guatemala). El Mirador was inhabited by around 100,000 people in its prime as a city.

Afterward, between the years 250 and 900, the classic period took place. In this period, there were many Mayan cities with between 50,000 and up to 120,000 inhabitants. It was also a period of great agricultural advancement, as the Mayans began to cultivate products such as beans and maize, in addition to acquiring an incredible degree of knowledge of astronomy.

As if that wasn't enough, during this period the Mayans developed a written language, in a moment in history when few peoples actually had one. This language was still in use when the Spaniards arrived, and samples of it can be found in ceramics, stelae, monuments, and more. It consisted of a series of glyphs, or symbols each representing a certain word, or syllable. The beauty of these glyphs lay in their nearly infinite potential to be made into any number of combinations, allowing any word to be subsequently written in any number of ways.

To these amazing accomplishments we must add an impressive knowledge of mathematics, as can be attested by the Mayan numerals that will be studied in this chapter shortly. A wonderful civilization indeed!

The third and final period, the post-classic period, lasted between the years 900 and 1539. Old cities that had been inhabited for as long as 2,000 years, were abandoned, and new cities emerged. The bulk of urban activity shifted from the south to the north, amidst a combination of blows that brought down the southern cities, such as war, disease, and natural disasters. After they were abandoned, Mayan cities just continued to deteriorate under the unstoppable power of nature, and were rediscovered centuries laters as the ruins covered in vegetation that were left.

Mayan Society and Urban Structure
Mayan Social Groups

There were four basic social groups among the Mayans, clearly distinguishable from one another as tends to happen with aboriginal Mesoamerican societies. The serfs were land workers at the service of landowners. The commoners, meanwhile, were farmers, workers, or servants living close to their land, outside of the city. Finally, the top social group, the nobility, "was for rulers, administrative officials, military commanders, high priests, and traders and they lived in urban centers." (Lipovac & Gradečki, 2018). As the same authors explain, these social groups were highly ordered within the city, which was distributed according to the numbers of people belonging to each category existing within it.

Mayan Urban Structure: the Main Buildings of a Mayan City

There were some architectural structures that simply couldn't fail to exist within a Mayan city. First of those structures, were the pyramids dedicated to religious activities; second, were the beautiful palaces where the nobles lived; the third, were the so-called observatories, a name given to certain circular temples dedicated to the god Kukulkán; and the fourth, were the ball courts. The ball game, sacred in Mesoamerica, will be discussed at more length in the next chapter; suffice it here to say that the Mayans held it in as sacred a place as the Aztecs, having inherited the tradition from the Olmecs.

For the purposes of getting in and out of the city, a causeway, or sacbe—consisting of an elevated paved road—could be used.

In addition to these public buildings, there were also residential buildings, in the form of huts. In the words of Lipovac and Gradecki (2018), these were "built of wooden poles and thatch, plastered with mud, set atop a low-height mound-base, and covered with hay that protected from sun and rain."

Some Mayan cities, though not all of them, also boasted city walls.

Chichén Itzá: An Example of a Mayan City

A wonderful example of a great Mayan city is Chichén Itzá, located in the Yucatán Peninsula. In it, one will be able to see a concrete example of the structure mentioned just above.

Its area is around five square kilometers, or nearly two square miles, and it contains a large number of beautiful buildings, made mainly of stone, that rested upon terraces. Those terraces were connected by a system of causeways, or saches, mentioned just above.

Among the important and prominent public buildings in Chichén Itzá, are buildings used for ritual purposes. El Castillo (the Castle) and the Temple of the Warriors may be classified as two such buildings. But, there were buildings with different functions as well, such as the circular Caracol, or the Snail, which seems to have been used as an astronomical observatory.

Chichén Itzá was also home to several ball courts, where the sacred game of ball was played, and of administrative buildings, as well as commercial ones—such as the Court of a Thousand Columns, which is believed to have been used as a marketplace.

The reader will see that the Mayan urban structure just delineated in this book, is present in the case of Chichén Itzá, including the fundamental buildings listed:

- pyramids such as El Castillo
- observatories such as El Caracol
- ball courts saches

As was the norm with Mesoamerican cities, Chichén Itzá depended on agriculture for its basic sustenance, but it also had access to water-based resources from the coastal waters near the city. In Chichén Itzá, the god Cha was the embodiment of the great power of water, an equivalent to the rain god Tláloc found in the central region of Mexico. The inhabitants of the city also depicted water plants, and animals to represent the god, and even to this day, the descendants of the Maya people still share a deep belief in these forces of nature. One example of these animals is the frog: several depictions of frogs could be found in the Cenote of Sacrifice, a place of high religious importance within the city; the frog is still linked to this day—in the minds of the modern-day Mayans—with rain. If a frog croaks, it is thought, then rain will come.

Deities such as the Sun God are also depicted in sacred places throughout Chichén Itzá. As also are deities of death and the Bacabs, creatures in charge of bearing the weight of the sky while the earth floated above the sea. Another important motif is the feathered serpent, called Kukulkán in the city of Chichén Itzá and the rest of the Yucatán Peninsula, equivalent of the god Quetzalcoatl of the central region of Mexico.

The Notable Mayan Numerals

A very interesting fact about the Mayans was their knowledge of mathematics. They had their own numerological system, which was base twenty. This means they counted objects twenty by twenty, just as we tend to use a base ten system and count ten by ten.

They used dots and lines to represent their numbers, and at some point (350 B.C.E. to the year 250) they even added a different symbol, for zero. Specifically, one dot was used to mean a value of one; a line represented five units; and zero units were represented by a symbol resembling a shell shaped like a turtle. To make the numbers in between, these symbols could be combined, as for example with three lines to make fifteen or one line and two dots to make seven.

Numbers were also written vertically, rather than horizontally, with the uppermost line containing the numbers between 0 and 20, the one below it reserved for numbers between 20 and 400, next for the numbers between 400 and 7,999, and so on.

It's worth mentioning here, how noteworthy it is that the Mayans actually had a symbol for zero. "Along with the Babylonian numerical system, this was the earliest known appearance of an explicit zero sign worldwide. At first, zero served to explain something that was absent in a particular calendar count, but later it got the numerical meaning used in calculations for more than 1,000 years."(Lipovac & Gradečki, 2018).

If the reader should choose to take a look for him or herself at the Mayan numerals, along with an illustrative example in the form of the Mayan depiction of the number 2018, he or she can do so by consulting the text Mayan cities of Yucatan, by Nenad Lipovac and Nikolina Gradečki, which features precisely such an illustration.

Mayan Astronomy

Just as it is about to become clear with the example of the calendar, the Mayan viewed astronomy too as something highly connected with the divine. It has to do with the gods, how they relate to one another, and how this affects our human lives. For example, the harvests, good or bad, are related to the gods of Rain and of the Sun. Plenty of human activities, from warfare to marriages, and sacrifices, were organized with the right astronomical moment in mind. The gods might be spoken about in terms we could use to describe our lives as humans: the moon is born every night and dies every morning. Gods interact with one another in a human way—which we can see in other mythologies too, such as the Greek and Roman ones.

The marked importance that astronomy had for the Mayans even implied that the very same event could be talked about both in an objective—or historical—way, or in an astronomical way. It is up to the expert reading the Mayan text to actually determine which of these two is true in any given instance, and—as the reader will certainly appreciate—the distinction between these two types of discourse may be tricky. The subject may seem rather trivial, but it is not devoid of significance: given the deep connection between history, astronomy, and mythology in the Mayan world, an error in this regard may produce a bigger misunderstanding of the whole picture that the archaeologist is trying to paint of this civilization. By contrast, understanding astronomical texts as such can greatly improve our understanding of the intricate correlations that have just been mentioned.

Fortunately, there are ways to deduce, with a fair amount of certainty, when a specific description of an event is actually astronomical.

In the first place, the expert must consider

whether or not the glyphs used in the text being studied are rare in non-astronomical texts while being used with more frequency in texts of known astronomical nature. If they do, then the text is probably an astronomical one.

He or she must also suspect the text of referring to its subject matter in the astronomical sense if the inscription makes reference to a point—very far in time, relative to when it was written—whether in the past or in the future, a point in time that could not have any meaning that directly applied to the writer's life.

Calculations that imply precise, astronomically charged intervals also make a text more likely to refer to an astronomical discourse, as do mentions made in the text to deities particularly associated with specific astronomical contexts or to ceremonies that typically occur in those types of contexts, or to dates that mark those contexts.

With this criteria, it is possible to determine the existence of texts primarily referring to astronomical matters—although not in a particularly great number. In the words of Kelley and Kerr (1973), "by these criteria, the number of primarily astronomical texts is not very large and even the number of dates is not impossibly great."

The Mayan Calendar

One great reason for the use of the numbers discussed at length above in this very chapter, is their use in the Mayan calendar. This is a very interesting and sophisticated calendar. In it, each day is assigned a number, one to thirteen, thus generating a thirteen-day period, or what in Spanish could be called a trecena (derived from trece, thirteen; just as a dozen means twelve, in Spanish docena, derived from the word for twelve, doce.) It is worth mentioning that the number 13 does not seem to be arbitrary here: all over Mesomerica, there was a prominent belief in Thirteen Heavens, dominating the important creation processes.

A day in the Mayan calendar does not have only a number; it also has associated with it one of twenty signs. A period of twenty days was called a uinal. The combination of trecenas, and urinals gives us 260 days in what we could call the Mayan "year", if we were to use our equivalent modern word. Even by present day Mayan descendants, this calendar is considered sacred, as it reflects uninterrupted divine creation. There is a word to describe this way to count the days: tzolkin (the Yucatec word), or tonalpouhalli (the Mexica word).

On top of this, we must consider that the Mayans also followed the cycles of Venus, and this meant that they knew how this astronomical cycle lined up with the sun's calendar year. Considering that one Venus cycle lasts 584 days, five whole Venus cycles will last a total of 2,920 days—which is exactly eight of our solar years. When these cycles aligned—once every five Venus years and eight solar years—Venus could be seen once more in the same position it occupied in the sky the last time the cycles aligned.

In addition to all mentioned above, we must always keep in mind that the Mayans did not view time the same way as we do. Their interest in the subject had to do with creation and cosmic energies. They wanted to understand the changes in these energies. They wanted to grasp their influence in creation in general, and in our own human lives in particular. This is the fascinating thing about this calendar: it has nothing to do with time as a physical thing and everything to do with it as a spiritual thing. Thus, it aimed to understand how their lives were going, what direction they were taking, and to serve as a prophetic calendar. This introduces another complication: the ritual calendar, which—as its name suggests—ordered the religious events in Aztec life.

The Ritual Calendar and the Tzolkin

Even when they had a notion of the solar year, the Mayans did not use it like we do. Instead, they used 260-day periods, which made up their sacred ritual calendar. This calendar was also used by other Mesoamerican cultures.

The way the Mayans kept track of time, within their ritual calendar, may be somehow familiar to how we count our days of the year: just as each day has a number and a month, the Mayans assigned a number and a sign to each day. Those symbols, as listed by Swedish defensor of Mayanism, Johan Carl Calleman (2004), were Alligator, Wind, Night, Seed, Serpent, Death, Deer, Rabbit, Water, Dog, Monkey, Road, Jaguar, Eagle, Vulture (or Owl), Earth, Flint, Rainstorm, and Light (or Lord). Calleman himself offers a complete list of these symbols, along with a little image of each one, and its Aztec counterpart. So if the reader should wish to see it, he or she need only consult Calleman's The Mayan Calendar and the Transformation of Consciousness. That list, or chart, was called tzolkin or tonalpouhalli.

The Long Count and End of the Mayan Calendar—(2012 and the "End of the World")

Besides the ritual calendar, the Mayans had another way to count time: the Long Count. Interestingly enough, this count is associated with the fabled "end of the world" that was supposed to happen in 2012.

The Long Count—to start by its very definition—is the way classical-era Mayans kept track of time in the long-term sense of the word. This count started, as most archaeologists agree today, on August 11, 3114 B.C.E. But, when does this calendar end? Well, it ends—or rather, ended—on December 21, 2012. This gives the Mayan calendar a total duration of 13 baktuns. Each baktun is 144,000 days long, just a bit under 394 of our common solar years and a half. In turn, each baktun may be divided into 400 tuns, with each tun lasting 360 days. The word tun means stone, and moving a stone was, in fact, a way to mark the changing of one tun into the next.

These are the temporal boundaries within which the Mayan Long Count may be situated.

CHAPTER 6
THE AZTEC CIVILIZATION — CITY STRUCTURE, SOCIETY, AND WARFARE

The Aztecs were agricultors, cultivating crops such as beans, squash, and maize. They worked hard to better the conditions for these crops: they dammed rivers where they needed to, in order to provide irrigation, they built stone terraces where the terrain was hilly. They even made fertile land out of swampy terrains by creating chinampas, rectangular plots of vegetation and sludge which floated above the water and produced a thick layer of soil secured in the edges by tree roots. Chinampas could form a network through which one could travel by canals. This gives us an idea of how notably advanced this civilization was, solving complex problems in a very ingenious way.

Aztec Cities and Their Basic Structure

The Aztecs did not function as a single unit,

but rather had different city-states, called altepetl. We could say that the capitals of these altepetls were a model for a typical Aztec city. In the construction of these cities, the Aztecs made the traditional Mesoamerican models their own by introducing their own innovations. But, there were still the basics that can be found in all of Mesoamerica: rectangular plazas with the civic buildings around them, constituting a sort of epicenter around which the rest of the city was built.

Around the epicenter, one could find neighborhoods in which the commoners and low-class nobility lived. The basic civic buildings were the usual ones to be found in Mesoamerica: pyramidal temples and other smaller shrines, ball courts, and palaces.

Aztec Pyramids

As far as public architecture goes, rectangular pyramids were certainly an important part of it. They could be dedicated to a very wide range of different gods. There were Aztec pyramids with one temple, and others with two. The first type, the single-temple pyramid, was the most common in Aztec times, while the two-templed pyramid was more common in the earlier period though it resurged in important cities such as the great

Tenochtitlán with its two-templed pyramid Templo Mayor (Major Temple).

Circular Temples and Small Altars

Not all Aztec temples had the shape of the rectangular pyramid: there were also circular temples, dedicated to the god of wind, Ehecatl. The Aztecs also built small altars throughout their cities, which can be found in other Mesoamerican cultures.

Ball Courts

The importance of ball games is not unique to the Aztecs, but shared with other Mesoamerican civilizations. The games were seen as representations of the movements and conflict between the moon, the sun, Venus, and other heavenly bodies. In the case of the Aztecs, ball games were also seen as a way to reenact warfare, with the losers being killed after the game—a custom which was lost after the Spanish conquest. In other words, the significance of these games was immense, and thus ball courts were an important architectural part of Aztec cities.

Ball could also be played just for fun, without such high stakes at play. There were amateur players, and professional ones, like we see in our modern sports, and there was even gambling over professional games.

The game was played between two teams, often with only two players in each team. The goal was to score points by passing the ball—made of solid rubber through hoops, or hitting markers located throughout the playing field. Like in our modern football, it was forbidden to play the ball with the hands: it was to be hit with the forearms or thighs.

Palaces

The royal palace was an important part of every altepetl. It was not only the place where the tlatoani lived with his family, but also a place for storing important goods, and to conduct important governmental meetings. Other palaces, alike in their design but smaller in size, were built by nobles with ranks below that of the tlatoani. All palaces shared a similar structure: a shrine for religious purposes, an opening to connect with the outside world opposite the shrine, and several rooms for both residential and political purposes on the sides. All this was structured around a courtyard, similarly to the way the main civic buildings of a city were structured around a plaza.

We can easily remark, as we make this overview of Aztec architecture, how religion permeated the whole structure of their cities, being an immensely important part of their lives.

Not Everybody is Created Equal: Aztec Social Classes

Within Aztec society, the first distinction we can make is that between the commoners, the vast majority of the population, and the elite classes, who held the power. Within each of these groups, we can find different subsets.

The lowest social class were the tlacotin, or slaves, who worked for other people who owned them. Aztecs did not have hereditary slavery, but rather took war prisoners and either sacrificed, or enslaved them. Above the tlacotin were the rest of the commoners, including some special categories of commoners. Two such categories are guild merchants, or pochtecas, and luxury artisans (sculptors, jewelers, and other similar craftsmen): people who could amass fair amounts of wealth through commerce.

Many products were manufactured by Aztec artisans, both daily use and luxury. Cotton textiles were among the most important of them, along with blades made of obsidian which could be used in a domestic environment, or to continue production. We must also keep in mind that every Aztec city had its marketplace. Marketplaces were very busy, and they made up an important part of the Aztec economy. Lacking money in our modern-day sense of the word, Aztecs could use products such as cacao beans to pay for cheaper purchases, and cotton textiles for more expensive ones.

Another special category of commoners was that of the higher ranks of the military and the priesthood.

Imperial, or city-state level officials denominated calpixque, who were in charge of tasks such as collecting taxes, were the other special group among the common people. These special groups could rank higher than the basic commoners in the social ladder, but were still considered commoners.

As for the nobility, there were also different types of noblemen, just as it happened with commoners. The highest rank of all was, of course, that of king, or tlatoani. The tlatoani ruled the respective city, or province, and his title was hereditary, just as it is with modern monarchies. Below the tlatoani were the lords, or teteuctin, who held important military, or political roles with varying degrees of importance and helped rule the commoners. A descendant of a lord or tecuhtli could hold the title of pilli (plural pipiltin), which meant the possibility of having a governmental position.

The Aztecs: Masters of Warfare
Life of a Soldier

The Aztecs took warfare, and the military in general, very seriously. In fact, distinguishing oneself as a soldier—taking many prisoners in battle—was one of the few ways in which an Aztec could climb up the social ladder. Military instruction, for boys whose fathers wanted them to follow that path, started at age fifteen. At this age, the father of the future soldier took him to the telpochcalli, or military school, as we could say. The priests of the telpochcalli had to accept responsibility for the child and his training. Another alternative, though typically reserved for boys of noble origin, was a type of military school, the calmenac. Training at the calmenac started earlier than in the telpochcalli (precise age is not clear), and covered not only military formation, but also intellectual education. When he reached the age of twenty, the young man could accompany the warriors in battle, and try to learn how to take captives. This was important, for he who did not achieve a capture was never to gain any military fame. This didn't need to necessarily happen the very first time the young man went to war, but eventual success was expected.

Of course, many went to war only as auxiliaries and had little to no real expectations of military fame—for them, this was not an issue. For those who succeeded in taking captives, became warriors. As a warrior, an Aztec could receive different rewards, both in material goods and in honors—such as rich clothes given to the soldier by the tlatoani. Jewelry was also a way to visually establish one's military rank, as was the haircut he wore and his war attire: what arms and armor he could wear, for example. The Aztecs also used face paint, as did many other Mesoamerican people, to signify their military rank. As an example, red and yellow were used to paint the face of a soldier when he made a capture.

The rewards would vary depending on the number of captives taken, and the perceived difficulty in capturing them. There were also changes throughout Aztec history.

Preparing for War

For the Aztecs, being ready for war, whenever it might come, was very important. In fact, war was simply a natural part of Aztec life, enough to grant supplying the army to be considered in the structure of every city. In fact, in every city, some portions of land, called milchimalli or cacalomilli, were designed to make sure war supplies were available. The tlatoani ordered every town under his power to send food and equipment to help the army. The help came from all over the empire—especially from the region closest to the capital of Tenochtitlan. As for arms, they were available in Tenochtitlan, in armories located both in the tlatoani's palace, and in the entrances to Tenochtoitlan's temple quartier. The name for this latter, large armory was the tlacochalco. Arms were even available in the city market, especially for the nobles, and other elite soldiers.

CHAPTER 7
THE INCAS — INHABITANTS OF THE ANDES MOUNTAINS

How the Incan Empire Came to Be: the Story of Pachacuti Inca Yupanqui

The Incas were a little different from the other civilizations we have been discussing in this book: their empire was located in South America, specifically in the Andes mountains. The center of operations, the capital of the Inca Empire, was the city of Cuzco, located in modern-day Peru. The Valley of Cuzco, which has an altitude of approximately 11,483 feet above sea level, lent its natural condition to this magnificent civilization. The valley itself can be found in the south-central Peruvian Andes, and Cuzco, the Incas capital, is found near the northern border of the valley.

From this location, the Incas expanded beyond their native Peru until they reached the modern-day countries of Bolivia, Ecuador, and

Chile. This is the civilization that the Spanish found upon their arrival in America: the largest state in the continent. This was due to the culmination of an expansion process starting from their origins in the Valley of Cuzco—but what gave rise to this Empire? Well, there's a story, still accepted by some today, that was recorded by the Spaniards themselves in times of the Conquest. It's the story of Pachacuti Inca Yupanqui.

The story goes something like this: one day the Incas were attacked by a rival tribe, the Chanca. The enemy targeted Cuzco itself, and Viracocha, leader of the Incas, ordered his people to flee the city. One of Viracocha's sons, Inca Yupanqui, decided then to take matters into his own hands: he seized power, and managed to defeat the Chanca by enlisting the help of other ethnic groups within the region. It was after this great victory that he decided to adopt the name of "Pachacuti", or "Transformer of the Earth". He simply took the throne from his father, although not without help from the grateful inhabitants of Cuzco, and gave rise to the Inca empire by simply waging war against whoever dwelled at the periphery of Inca territory. By doing this, they expanded the area under effective Inca rule to double what it once was.

The Inca Religion: Gods and Huacas

With conquests such as the Incas made, came a serious question: how do you treat those who succumb to you? In other words,what kind of a relationship do you build with them? Of course, it seems reasonable to think that one wants to establish, with absolute clarity and certainty, one's domain over whoever one has conquered; but it's just as logical to want to have a peaceful environment, and therefore to want cordial relations. The Incas decided to take the latter approach when it came to religion. Any group of people that was conquered by the Incas, had to give up any gods they may have revered that contradicted the Incan religion; but as long as no such contradiction was present, they were allowed to continue worshiping their own deities. The Incas themselves adopted gods from conquered peoples and made them their own, although never with such intensity as their own gods. This was not exactly done out of any particular concern, or respect for their defeated enemies; but it did serve as an intelligent tactic to maintain their control over them, as was their primary objective.

That being said, who were these Inca gods? Well, like many similar cultures, the Incas saw the divine in nature, therefore adoring as divinities many natural phenomena. Let us now take a look at their Parthenon. Specifically we're going to look at the four major gods—Viracocha, Inti, Mama Quilla, and Illapa.

Viracocha

First, we have the creator known by many names such as Ticci Viracocha (Divine Origin), Illa Tecce ("Eternal light", "sacred origin"), or Pachayachachic ("Instructor of space and time"). For the sake of simplicity, we will name him Viracocha. He was tall, dressed in white, and gave each ethnic group its defining cultural traits, from language and songs, to foods and clothing. It is said—in the Inca creation myth, or at least a version of it— that Viracocha created humankind out of the stones found on the shore of lake Titicaca, out of which he emerged. Before creating humans, he created giants; but he later destroyed them.

He is mentioned in nearly all major Inca festivals, although he had no particular major ceremony centered around him. He had a temple dedicated to him in Cuzco, called Quishuar Chancha, and another located between Cusco and lake Titicaca, called Raqchi.

The Sun: Inti

Another major Inca god was Inti, the Sun, protector, and emblem of the whole empire. Unlike Viracocha, Inti did have a ceremony dedicated to him: the Inti Raymi, which took place annually to mark the solstice in June. The Coricancha, the main temple in Cuzco, had a representation of Inti through a statue of a boy, Punchao (the day), made of gold and life-sized. The Incas believed that Inti shared a sacred bond with the Inca royalty, and to symbolize that, when an emperor died, his internal organs were reduced to ashes which were in turn placed in Punchao's belly.

The worship of Inti was presided over by the high priest, or Vilahoma, of noble origin. His assistants, consecrated virgins called acllas, inhabited the "House of the chosen women" or acllahuasi, located next to the coricancha.

The Moon: Mama Quilla
The wife of the Sun was the Moon, Mama Quilla. She too had a representation in the Coricancha: a statue of a woman, life-sized just like Punchao. She also had a temple devoted to her in Lake Titicaca, where many people came to worship her, represented by a statue made of gold and silver, and life-sized just as the one in the Coricancha.

She was also the protector of the women of the empire.

The Thunder: Illapa
Illapa was the god of thunder, an inhabitant

of the sky. He had the power to produce rain by getting water from the river in the sky that was—for the people of the Andes, including the Incas—the milky way. So, if rain was needed, Illapa was the god to pray to in order to get it.

His clothing was golden, and it could flash when he ran, which produced lighting; meanwhile, by cracking his sling—which he held on one hand, while in the other the held a war club—he could produce thunder.

The temple of Pukamarka, in Cuzco, contained a shrine dedicated to Illapa.

The Huacas

The huacas, revered throughout the Andean region, were a manifestation of some sort of superhuman entity, or power. It was believed by the Andeans, that people were created by their personal huaca, not from scratch, but as a source of continued vitality and identity somehow reminiscent of the breath of life God gives to man, which puts man apart from the rest of creation. In gratitude for this, sacrifices were offered to the huaca.

A whole human group could have a common huaca as their creator, or camac. Even animal species could have a huaca.

Practically anything could be identified as a

huaca: a shrine, an effigy, a mountain, an oracle, or a mummy. As long as the energy of the supernatural was there, that object— whatever it was—was a huaca.

Mummification

One very interesting aspect of Inca culture and religion, was their tradition to mummify the bodies of important and powerful people, to be buried along with their personal items. We must understand that Andean cultures, just as we have seen with Mesoamerican ones, believed in a continued existence after death and in a communication between this terrenal plane, and the afterlife. Thus, one's deceased ancestors deserved gifts and honors, which in turn could mean a more prosperous life on Earth for those who gave the gifts. The process of mummification was just a part of the treatment the Incas, and other Andeans gave the dead as still-present beings. Unfortunately, Incan tombs are practically nonexistent today due to human intervention.

Confession

Andean people actually practiced personal confession of one's sins to a priest. It was even a public duty, because it was believed that misfortunes to the community could arise if the sins of its members were not duly in the open and atoned for by fasting, receiving a whipping, or perhaps being temporarily exiled from the community. Such was the capital importance of confession, that it was to be done at least annually; and if a penitent did not confess to all of his or her sins, he or she could receive a beating in the back with a stone administered by the confessor.

The most interesting thing here is the fundamental difference that we may find between confession as we see in the case of the Andean people and confession as the Christian religion presents it to us: the outward versus inward focus of it. For a Christian, it's the eternal destiny of his or her soul that's at stake when confessing—and, in general, when being a good Christian. In the case of an Andean native, such as an Inca, it's the community that needs him or her to confess in order to remain healthy and happy.

A question that is somehow related to this is, what is to be confessed? More specifically, does one confess only sinful acts, or also sinful thoughts? Of course, the right answer from the point of view of a Christian would be both. Regarding the Andean people, the sources are divided. Some say that the Incas did not consider their sinful thoughts and desires as proof that they were barbaric, and others say that they actually did attach importance to those matters, a proof of their more civilized status.

Machu Picchu: the Lost city of the Inca

A mere 70 miles from Cusco, capital of the Incan empire, a real archaeological treasure can be found: the so-called lost city of the Inca, Machu Picchu, meaning "old peak" in the tongue of the Incas, Quechua. This lost city lies at quite an elevation of 7.710 ft above sea level. Below it lies the Urubamba river, and there is also forest; but Machu Picchu cannot be seen from those locations.

The city was used as a residence for the Imperial family, especially during the winter, and for their servants, and advisors.

After being effectively abandoned for around 400 years, Yale assistant professor Hiram Bingham found Machu Picchu again in 1911, and today it remains one of the most famous tourist attractions of Perú. What professor Bingham uncovered was a set of 150 or 200 buildings, some of which were sacred temples, and a terraced zone dedicated to agricultural use. The whole complex, measuring around five square miles, was home to around 1,000 people in the days it was most populated. Its different sections were connected by an impressive set of stairways.

Machu Picchu, a Legacy of Pachacuti

One of the most influential of the Inca rulers, Pachacuti—protagonist of the legend of how the Incas became an empire—held the power between 1438 and 1471. He had Machu Picchu built between 1460 and 1470, perhaps as a means to celebrate the Inca victory against the Chancas which the legend tells about.

The Many Architectural Wonders of Machu Picchu

Apart from the Inca palace that can be found in the complex, there are several other interesting architectural landmarks in Machu Picchu.

There were four temples in the complex: two of them—the Main Temple and the Temple of the Three Windows—were located next to the residence of the priest, and the other two—the Temple of the Condor and the Temple of the Sun—were both near the Inca palace. The Temple of the Sun was adjacent to the royal tomb, and it had two very carefully placed windows, which looked directly into the sunrise on the two yearly solstices—summer and winter.

There was also a prominent main plaza, in front of which the Main Temple was situated. To one side of the Temple, there was the Temple of the Three Windows and the priest's house just beside it; and to the other side, there was the Intiwuatana. It's not clear whether the Intiwuatana, or "hitching post of the sun", was a sacrificial altar, or a solar clock, or even a dial that helped determine the position of the sun during solstice; but its importance to the Incas remains unquestioned. The existence of both the Intiwuatana and the solstice-oriented windows of the Temple of the Sun are a testimony to the knowledge possessed by the Incas on the subject of astronomy, a trait shared by the Mesoamerican cultures studied in this book.

On the other side of the city, beyond the city gates, there was a cemetery, and a guardhouse, along with other five barracks—located at the other side of the agricultural terraces—that may have served as a watchtower.

We may appreciate the similarities between the layout of this Inca city and the one of the ancient Mesoamerican cities. In both cases there is a main plaza in a privileged position; and there is a great importance attached to religious buildings, such as temples. Likewise, in both cases the royal palace featured prominently within the scope of the city. Even the use of a certain patch of land to grow crops was a common trait between Incas, and other Measoamericans. We can therefore say that the main functions within the city were similar between the Incas and the other Mesoamerican cultures.

CHAPTER 8
THE SPANISH CONQUEST — HERNAN CORTES AND THE FALL OF THE AZTECS

Mesoamerica: What the Spanairds Saw, Their Treatment of the Natives, and the Great Debate

Before we talk of the arrival of Hernán Cortés and the subsequent fall of the Aztec Empire, let us paint a general picture of what the Spaniards saw upon arriving in the Americas, and how they reacted to this new world that they were discovering.

What the Spaniards found in the Americas was vastly different from all that they had previously known, and they were absolutely fascinated by it all. They were also rather defensive, because the whole way in which they viewed the world was challenged. Among the new questions that arose with this whole new world now appearing before them was a particularly burning one: what status did the natives have? In other words, were they even human just like the Europeans were? As Europe was the cultural center of the world at the time, and in a way the epitome of the civilized world, such a question—unimaginable in our present day—was bound to come up. Unfortunately, none of the answers the Europeans gave to it was in the least flattering for the natives.

At the beginning, there were two basic ways in which the Europeans viewed the natives: either as "noble savages" who were still uncorrupted by the vices of civilization and were in need of saving by being converted into Christianity, or as "wild people", human in race but half animalistic in their behavior, and therefore not quite human in the full sense of the word. Slowly, with time and continued contact between these clashing cultures, a third view appeared, that of the indigenous people simply being inhabitants of a completely different world, a world to be studied and understood by learning about it. Only with study, thought the Spaniards who took this stance, could they determine exactly what the nature of the natives was, as well as their place in Creation, in civilization, etc.

The fact that the natives were considered to

be so fundamentally different from the Europeans led to a very poor treatment of them, and the subject prompted in 1550 a summons by Spanish King Charles V to the Council of the Fourteen, in Valladolid, Spain, to settle the matter. Specifically, the goal was to determine, once and for all, what the nature of the natives was, and whether the Spanish Crown had any right whatsoever to convert them to Christianity and turn them into servants of the Crown, even if that meant using violence—and, if yes, where that right derived from. This became what we call the Great Debate.

Juan Ginés de Sepúlveda, a Spanish philosopher, argued for one side that the Indians—as the Spaniards called them—were naturally inferior to the Europeans, and as such deserved a perpetually inferior position in society. Bartolomé de las Casas, a Dominican priest, countered for the other side that, in his experience as the Bishop of Chiapas and minister in Mayan communities, natives were indeed rational. They should be converted to Christianity, but there was no need of violence for that—only persuasion. Sadly, not even Las Casas had a real, deep understanding, or appreciation for the natives just as they were, with their own culture and world views. He too considered them simply as prospective future

Christians, with their best quality being precisely that: potential, and the quality they shared with actual Christians. The natives were also denied the possibility of being physically present in the debate through an actual representative.

In that sense, the expeditions that arrived in America, such as Hernán Cortés' own, had one main goal, and one alone: to convert the natives to Christianity. It might help the reader, in trying to understand this, to think that for the Spaniards to see an indigenous culture with religious beliefs such as are mentioned in this book was simply to see souls headed for hell. In fact, a Spaniard who did not care about the soul of a native—even a single one—might be sinning and meriting an eternity in hell himself. What is curious about this situation is that, while faith was all-important, we could say that the moral principles that are supposed to lie underneath faith did not matter nearly as much. The goal of converting the natives was to be reached at literally any cost, even by violent means if necessary, negating—at least for this instance— the ideal of refraining from causing others harm. The Spaniards were also operating on the belief that dying in the Faith meant dying in the Lord regardless of what the person had been like while alive, just to press again the point of how important this was to the conquerors, Cortés obviously included.

As a sort of example of the Europeans' methods, let the reader cast the following image in his or her mind, from the times of the expedition led by Cortés. The inhabitants of Cozumel, in the Yucatan era, were asked to let go of their idols by the Christian missionaries. Those idols were to be destroyed. The horrified natives warned that the gods that sent sunshine and storm would certainly retaliate in the event of such a blasphemous act. Cortés simply ordered the destruction of the idols, simply thinking that the very fact that the natives' fear wouldn't come true would eventually convince them of the error of their beliefs.

Cortés Arrives in the Americas

Hernán Cortés arrived in the Americas as a young man in 1504, one of many Spaniards who came to the West Indians to be settlers, and hopefully acquire quick and easy riches. He arrived specifically to the island of Hispaniola, or "Little Spain", which we now know has Haiti. He spent years in Hispaniola, working some lands that he was given, and in 1511 joined Diego de Velásquez in his expedition to Cuba. Velásquez had been ordered to start a Spanish settlement in Cuba, a territory yet to be explored, and Cortés joined the expedition. The efforts were succesful, and Cortés spent several years in Cuba, becoming one of the great landlords of the island. After the campaign to conquer Cuba, he was made Velasquez' chief secretary; and he ended up as Magistrate of Santiago, the most important town on the island. During this time in Cuba, he participated in several exploratory trips to various parts of the American continent. It was during one of these trips that the Spaniards learned of the inhabitants of Mexico, more sophisticated and civilized than the other tribes they had come across until then.

First Spanish Ventures to Mexico

As fate would have it, the Spaniards were to arrive in Mexico not long after, on an expedition that was originally headed for the Bahama Islands. This expedition sailed on February 8, 1517 and was led by Hidalgo Hernández de Córdoba. Due to problems faced along the journey, Hernández de Córdoba and his men ended up on the Mexican coast, specifically in Yucatán.

Upon arriving, the expedition came face to face with the Mayans. Their cultural level was astonishing: they were mathematicians and astronomers, actually better than any other culture in the world at that time. They had great cities made of stone, and sophisticated expressions of art in the form of pieces of pottery, paintings, buildings, and more. This advanced cultural level couldn't pass unnoticed by the Spaniards, who also took note of the well-cultivated land and the fine use of cotton to make clothing. Unfortunately, the natives were not inclined to receive the Spaniard with open arms, but rather with hostility and mistrust; but the report he was able to give when the expedition returned to Cuba some months later was interesting enough to grant another visit.

Juan de Grijalva, nephew of Velásquez, was sent next with his own expedition by order of his uncle. Fortunately, being forewarned about the unfriendly nature of the natives, he was able to be considerably better equipped to face them than his predecessor had been. He was able to secure an interview with the Aztec leader, which, although made difficult by the difference in languages, yielded results. Presents were interchanged, and in Grijalva's case, that meant receiving vessels, jewels, and golden ornaments. After this successful encounter, Grijava continued his exploration of the new territory; but he sent a man, Alvarado, back to Cuba with the riches and reports of what had been found. When Velásquez heard the news Alvarado had to tell him, he decided that it was definitely worth it to proceed to subjugate the recently discovered region. With that in mind, he set out to get the necessary authorization for another expedition, and decided Hernán Cortez was the man to lead it. And so, on November 18, 1518 Cortés departed on his conquering mission.

Once in America, the first goal of the Spaniards, as we have established, was to convert the natives to Christianity. But, in order to do that, and actually in order to achieve any communication, the Spaniards needed some help. The native language was unknown to them, and it was posing a serious problem. Fortunately, Cortés recruited a slave, a young native that could adequately understand both parties, to act as an interpreter and bridge the gap. The Spaniards called her Marina. She was well liked by all, serving the Spaniards well and being at the same time highly empathic with the natives. As for Cortés, his appreciation of her grew more and more, so much so that he turned her from his interpreter, to his secretary and then, eventually, his mistress and mother of his son Martín.

On the Way to the Aztec Ruler: the Encounter Between Cortés and Moctezuma's Governor

Having, then, the assistance he needed,

Cortés could finally establish a proper communication method with the natives. The locals introduced themselves as subjects of the Mexican Empire, ruled by the powerful Moctheuzoma—Moctezuma in westernized spelling. As for the province they were in, it was governed by a noble named Teuhtitle. Cortés, in turn, introduced himself, and his people as friendly visitors who would like to speak with the Aztec governor. And so it was arranged, and Teuhtitle reunited with Cortés. The Spaniard expressed his will to see Moctezuma, in order to personally deliver to him the presents he and his men, envoys of a powerful king who ruled beyond the seas, had brought as a sign of their complete goodwill. The native governor replied that the presents would be brought to the Emperor, and then, if he decided he wanted to see the Spaniards, he would inform them. Presents were exchanged as one could expect, and the Aztec delegation departed the Spanish camp.

Some time after this encounter with Moctezuma's governor, the Spaniards would, at last, meet the Emperor himself.

Capture and Death of Moctezuma

Cortés and his men were finally able to meet Moctezuma, and were actually welcome in the great city of Tenochtitlán as hosts. They were lodged in the castle of Moctazuma's father, Axaccayatl, and visits were exchanged between Cortés and the Aztec ruler in both of their dwellings. Cortés decided not to push the idea of religious conversion to the Emperor, at least for the time being. A peaceful coexistence between natives and foreigners ensued.

The problem was that, while Cortés and his men had managed to get into Tenochtitlán, they had not actually conquered it, which was what they had ultimately come to do. To remedy this unfortunate state of events, Cortés decided that Moctezuma should be captured, whether by being convinced to come to the Spanish dwelling voluntarily, or by force if needed. Naturally the natives would not dare attack the Europeans if that would mean their own ruler was in danger by this act. The Spaniards could rule using the Emperor as a sort of symbolic image, which would greatly help the conquerors in their mission.

It was hard to convince Moctezuma to leave his palace and accompany the Spaniards to the one they were inhabiting, but it was managed during a visit Cortés and some of his men paid to Moctezuma in his palace in 1519. Cortés took advantage of the death of some of his men, which had occurred just prior: certainly, if Moctezuma was innocent in the matter, residing with the Spaniards until a full investigation could be made would contribute to establish his innocence! After repeatedly protesting the degradation this effectual imprisonment would mean to him—even offering his children to go instead of him—and being just as repeatedly reassured of the utmost respect he would receive, Moctezuma finally followed the Spaniards to their quarters, while the stunned Aztec nobles looked on.

Moctezuma's life with the Spaniards was a comfortable one: he was given whatever chambers he preferred, and he could go about his daily life much as he did before. He was under supervision of Spanish soldiers, though, and considerable efforts were made to convert him to Christianity, though to no avail. He eventually did recognize the authority of the Spaniards, though, and went as far as asking his own people to respect and obey them as they had him. Many riches were also given to the Europeans.

Meanwhile, things didn't stay calm for long. Battles were still to be fought, as the Aztecs weren't about to idly sit and wait while the newcomers just turned their whole lives upside down. It was in one of these riots that Moctezuma received a wound to the temple that would eventually kill him in 1520. With Moctezuma dead, and therefore unable to use him as a secret weapon to control the Aztecs, Cortés and his men abandoned Tenochtitlán.

Final Fall of Tenochtitlán

Approximately one year after the death of Moctezuma, in 1521, the Spanish returned to Tenochtitlán, and this time, they were ready to unleash all of their might. A series of attacks, one after the other, were launched upon the city. The palace of Axayacatl, where the Spaniards once had dwelled, was burnt down. So was the palace of Moctezuma. And so began an arduous battle of strengths: the Spaniard did as much damage as they could, and by the time they attacked again, the Aztecs had repaired a considerable amount of the damage done, trying to keep up. The capital was sieged for long and arduous months until, finally, it fell. Guatemozin, who was then the leader of the Aztecs, surrendered, and the Aztecs fled the city.

Cortés would continue to have many more adventures; but the conquest of Mexico was certainly one of his most prominent military triumphs.

CHAPTER 9
MESOAMERICAN RELIGION: A MULTIPLICITY OF GODS

It is a nearly impossible task to try to count all of the gods of the Mesoamerican pantheon, across all the cultures that inhabited the region. But there are certain common traits among those gods, and it's important to draft those traits before devoting a few lines to some of those gods in particular.

First of all, Mesoamerican gods can be divided into two different groups. The first group, is what we can call creator gods; and the second, the tribal gods, venerated in some specific city, or village, and acting as protector of said place and its people but with no role in the act of creation of the world.

Secondly, Mesoamerican gods tend to represent some force of nature. Mesoamericans attached great importance to all things related to the way nature worked, and they explained its powers in terms of religion. The gods also had a hand in human life and activities, hence the need to keep them contented. They were the link between humankind and nature, between this world and the next. Much like the monotheistic religions prevalent today depict God, except with a deep emphasis in the forces of nature—probably derived from the lack of the scientific answers we can nowadays give to natural phenomena.

Thirdly, Mesoamerican gods did not only represent natural phenomena: they also had a specific image to represent them, and a set of anthropomorphic characteristics. In this regard, they were similar to the Greek, or Roman gods, who were depicted as having human attributes and personalities while being explicitly in charge of things like the thunder such as Zeus and the tides of the ocean such as Poseidon, etc. Gods even formed a hierarchy, more or less reflecting the human hierarchy of the people who venerated them, as Pedro Carrasco wrote in reference to the Aztec society and gods, and was cited by Florescano (1997.). Each one had his or her own cult and his or her own identity.

The Creation Gods

Creation gods have the task of creating the world as we know it from the chaos that existed before it. Typically they are depicted as a couple, representing between them all aspects, masculine and feminine, of creation. In this sense, there was a sexual element to the Mesoamerican cosmogony, with the earth representing the feminine principles and characteristics, and heaven having the masculine ones.

From this powerful couple, the rest of the gods and the rest of creation is born. The way the gods are organized and ranked parallels the way human society works.

The Tribal Gods

Tribal gods were venerated in specific cities, or villages. They were anthropomorphic, as all gods tended to be, but they also had some characteristics shared with the natural world, which linked the respective god with the natural element in some important way. For example, a particularly strong deity could be represented with some resemblance to a strong animal, such as a jaguar, to symbolize the common attribute of strength.

These deities also represented the values the people who adored them held most highly and that they most wanted to pass unto the future generations. The most important activities, natural resources and, in general, aspects of human life were linked to these gods.

They lead human lives, but extraordinary ones, worthy of unusual praise, like defeating the enemies of their people. In general, acts of high importance to their people were prominent in the life of these deities: a tribal god could be responsible for a people to have been able to prosper into a successful kingdom, for them to have acquired their characteristic traits that identified them as a people, and other similar feats.

Some Specific Gods
Quetzalcoátl
Quetzalcoatl is a dual being, as we can note by his very name, which derives from the Nahua words quetzalli, meaning "precious green feathers"—being, we may infer, the feathers of a beautiful bird—and coatl, meaning "serpent". This is not only a dual nature, but also a nature representing the duality of opposites: while the bird symbolizes Heaven, place of fertility, and order, the serpent symbolizes Earth, in which the cycle of life, generation, and destruction takes place. These forces are antagonistic and battle each other: light and darkness, life and death, day and night.

Quetzalcoatl may also be depicted as a man, specifically a white man. Various Mesoamerican civilizations talk of "white gods", white bearded men who arrived in America and gave the natives all they needed to prosper. Quetzalcoatl was one of those white gods, the one whose legend actually lives on. He goes by different names: Quetzalcoatl is his Toltec and Aztec name, the Mayans called him Kukulkan. Even the Incas had their own version of Quetzalcoatl, called Viracocha.

The legend talks of a Toltec king, precisely named Quetzalcoatl, who held power between the years 977 and 999. He was a great king, wise, and prudent, but fell into bad habits, coerced by a demon. Ashamed of this, he left his country. Many years later, he was on the coast, and here the legend divides into different variations: he may have died at sea, with his heart transforming into the morning star, or he went back where he came from, by boat, promising to return. It is said that the Aztecs might have taken Hernán Cortés, upon his arrival at México, to be Quetzalcoatl himself, returning as he had promised.

The Agricultural Gods of Teotihuacán
In Mesoamerica, deities frequently represented nature and natural phenomena. A perfect example of this is Teotihuacán, the main gods of which were agricultural ones. The main

agricultural goddess of Teotihuacán is the Goddess of the Cave, with her great powers of fertility, capable of gifting life, and determining death. She was always accompanied by Tláloc, a masculine deity, bringer of thunder, lightning, and rain; as well as by the Plumed Serpent, associated with the regeneration of nature, and of the vegetal world.

Another god related to agriculture was the Aztec god of rain, Tlaloc. He's represented in post-classic codices, and also on stone sculptures. His image is typically that of a pair of eyes, a lip with fangs protruding from them, and rings surrounding them. Other representations of the god are images of a person, with the fanged lip just mentioned, pouring water from a vessel in one hand and holding an adze and a serpent, symbols of lightning, in the other. This second type of representation appears in a restored version of an ancient Mexican Codex Borgia. If the reader of this book should be interested in studying this document, he or she can do so by reading The Codex Borgia: a Full-Color Restoration of the Ancient Mexican Manuscript, by Gisele Díaz and Alan Byland.

It bears keeping in mind that several rain deities are represented in Teotihuacán iconography. The name Tlaloc may be used to identify many of them. A great effort has been made by archaeologists to help identify each of the deities more precisely, and separate what can be considered a genuine version of Tlaloc from other separate entities.

Here we might say that experts face precisely the opposite problem of that found in the case of Quetzalcoatl: instead of having a single deity being depicted in very different forms, we have what seem to be different deities being depicted in very similar ways. If one thinks that both of these problems must be taken into account when doing archaeological work, and identifying the artistic representations found in the pieces of art the expeditions unearth, we can see how difficult, and delicate it is to be able to say with confidence exactly what is represented. Unfortunately, we don't have the possibility of talking to the people who made the pieces of art!

Venus

Venus had a strong divine presence in Mesoamerica. Mesoamericans, and Mayans in particular, were always looking to the sky and keeping record of the phenomena they could observe; and they came to draw interesting conclusions from those observations.

They noted, for example, that Venus had five

periodical revolutions, which coincided with eight annual revolutions of the Earth around the Sun. They saw Venus transform throughout the year, appearing in two different forms each visible in its own time of the year. There was also a time in which Venus wasn't visible; and, that was precisely eight days, which is the time it took for a corn seed to sprout from the ground. In other words, Venus represented life, death, and resurrection. It was the Morning Star, associated with light and its triumph over death, as well as with warriors; and, the Evening Star, associated with fertility but also with death. In the Popol Vuh, sacred book of the Quiché Mayan people (the Mayans from Guatemala), the Morning and Evening Stars were represented by the divine twins Xalanqué and Hunahpú, respectively.

Venus was strongly associated with the cyclical aspect of the calendar and with the agricultural cycle of sowing and reaping.

It was nocturnal Venus that led the Sun to its demise at night, and it was morning Venus that tried to defeat the new Sun every morning and failed, leaving the new Sun to reign.

The Sun

The Sun was another important force that Mesoamerican people recognized and revered.

Every morning at dawn, the new sun illuminated the Earth, extending its benign influence upon it, washing away the forces of the night until it came to its zenith at noon. Later in the day, the afternoon sun began its descent until it perished in the netherworld at midnight.

Maize, a Sacred Element

For the Mesoamerican cultures studied within this book, maize was not only a very important part of their diet: it was also sacred. The Aztecs, for example, had a goddess of maize, and of sustainment, called Coatlicue, which translates from nahuátl to something like "serpent that uses a skirt". The original nahuátl words are coatl, serpent, and cue, skirt. She manifested in different ways, representing the maize plant in the different stages of its life cycle: Xilonen was the deity of young maize, Centeotl was her equivalent for ripe maize, and finally Ilamatecihuatl was the goddess of old maize.

In the Peninsula of Yucatán, the Mayans had a masculine representation of the god of maize. He is depicted as young, often with maize growing out of his body. His head has a very peculiar shape. In the case of a certain ceramic plate, daring from the early classic period, and found in the state of Campeche, this god has wings in his arms and wears a jaguar's skin as his underwear. An image of this beautiful plate may be found in Symbolism and Use of Maize in Pre-Hispanic and Colonial Religious Imagery in Mexico, by Eva Benítez, should the reader wish to take a look at it.

A Mesoamerican culture that inhabited Mexico between approximately 1200 and 1521 and that is not studied in this book, the Tarascan people, also had a goddess of maize. She was called Xaratanga, and her husband was the sun of the underworld. She was also associated with Caricaueri, god of fire, in a duality that allows for life, death, and rebirth.

In addition to all of this, and as the reader will learn in more detail in the next chapter of this book, the sacred book Popol Vuh tells about the attempts the gods made to create humankind, and the attempt that finally ended in success was the one that used maize as the main element to build their bodies. This aligns perfectly with the great importance given to maize in Mesoamerican culture.

The Importance of Cacao

Along with corn, cacao—in its liquid form to be consumed as a drink, as well as presented as pods, seeds, or balls of cacao—certainly had a major role in the life of Mesoamerican people, so much so that it even reached divine status. In fact, the Popol Vuh, sacred book of the Quiché Mayan people, mentions Cacao Woman, a goddess of cacao. Some figurines found in Guatemala, corresponding to the late Classic period, have cacao pods growing from their bodies. Masculine versions of this kind of figure have also been found.

Cacao appears to also be important to the gods in the sense of being wanted and highly valued by them. Cacao is mentioned as a sacred tree, and as a food source predating the creation itself, capable of bringing balance between the Earth, the Sky above it, and the Underworld beneath it.

There are also instances of victims of human sacrifice being depicted wearing strings of cacao pods round their necks, another proof of the importance of this product for the Mesoamerican people. The book Chocolate: Pathway to the gods, by Dreiss and Greenhill, contains beautiful illustrations referring to the link between cacao, and divinity mentioned here, should the reader want to see them.

In the Mesoamerican world, cacao was used as a currency and as a high value commodity. It certainly had a great economical importance. But it was also highly appreciated for its taste and the benefits that it was said to have for the human body and soul. The consumption of cacao by indigenous Mesoamerican goes as far back as 1500 B.C.E, perhaps even beyond that. It is also important to mention that the health of the cacao tree leads to a healthy overall ecosystem—and vice versa—which serves as an example of how Mesoamerican religious thinking worked: even without the vast knowledge about biodiversity and conservation that we have at our disposal today, these civilizations seemed to understand the importance of this tree, and they attributed this importance to the gods.

CHAPTER 10
MESOAMERICAN MYTHOLOGY — CREATION STORIES AND HERO TALES

Myths: Why They Are Real and How They Are Depicted

When we think about a myth, we might think of it as some made-up story. Something that simply isn't true. But, that popular use of the expression does not apply to actual mythology, such as what we are going to discuss here. A true myth, one that's an actual part of a mythology—is essentially true. It's an actual depiction of the way a certain community views, and understands the world. Beyond the magical creatures, or impossible feats that they depict, there is always a grain of truth in them. A myth can provide an actual explanation to a phenomenon that we otherwise cannot make sense of—and this is very important, considering that we must understand the world in order to navigate it day by day. In that sense, a myth is profoundly real because, by impacting our understanding of the world and our behavior within it, it actually impacts the world itself. We can act upon the world and change it, all based on a myth that is deeply important and significant to us.

Another thing that we may usually think about myths is that they are stories that one hears, or perhaps reads. But a myth can take on many different forms: it may be told orally, written, painted, or sung. It can even be represented in the construction of a building. Mythical themes and stories can take on many forms and manifestations. This was certainly true in the case of Mesoamerica.

For example, Mesoamerican pottery often has a mythical significance, usually used as part of rituals. These pieces of pottery depicted deities and myths. Sculptures are another source of mythical manifestations. There are also codices, ancient books painted in paper made of bark, or deerskin. In these codices we can find calendars, description of rituals, the history of a town, etc. Instead of writing, the Mesoamerican used pictographs, and sometimes phonetic elements. Seventeen of these codices are still in existence.

Mesoamerica: Worlds Created, Worlds Destroyed

The question of how the world was created was one that ancient Mesoamericans certainly posed to themselves, and there are several stories that try to answer that question.

A key difference between the western religious version of creation, and the Mesoamerican one, is that we view the world as having one singular creation and one singular story, whereas the Mesoamerican civilizations believed in the creation of several worlds, of several eras of the world. The one we live in is just that, one of many. Worlds begin and worlds end, to be replaced by the next one. In that sense, the Mayan Long Count, mentioned in Chapter 5, is one of many Long Counts—just the one corresponding to the world the Mayans happened to live in. The end of the Long Count they were using, the one that ended in 2012, might just mean the start of a new world.

The Popol Vuh and the Creation of the World and Humanity

The Popol Vuh is the sacred book of the Quiché Mayan people, and it contains the story of how the world—and humanity—came to be created. It's through the analysis of this text that we will take a glimpse into Mesoamerican cosmogony.

In this beautiful text, we are told of a placid, inert Primordial World in which nothing moves, or makes a sound. There are only the gods Quetzal Serpent and Sovereign, also referred to as "she who has borne children" and "he who has begotten sons". There is also the deity "Heart of Sky". From that primordial world, by a collective and well thought out process of collaboration between the aforementioned gods, the earth was made. After the earth came the animals, to inhabit mountains, and forests. The gods wanted the animals to worship them, but the animals couldn't bring themselves to talk, and thus couldn't satisfy their creators: so they decided to create someone who could, and would, worship them as they wanted. The animals were relegated to forests and canyons, and the gods, feeling that they had failed in their mission to create creatures who could speak their names and worship them, decided to try again.

This first part of the text is not too far removed from the story we find in the beginning of the Genesis book of the Bible, with one notable distinction: the Christian God did not want the animals to worship Him, like the Popol Vuh gods did. The only creature that the Christian God puts above all the rest and orders to follow His command, are humans. And moreover, the Christian God saw that everything He created was good.

The gods of the Popol Vuh then tried to create a man out of mud precisely to fulfill that role, without success: the mud didn't make a solid, resistant body, but a frail, and weak one. A second attempt was made to make men as wooden effigies: and they could talk, walk, and multiply like the mud man couldn't do. But these wooden effigies had no true heart, no true understanding. So they, too, were exterminated. Then a third creation of man came about: the man made of maize, and we could consider it the "successful" one.

The Popol Vuh tells us that maize was used to create four men, with water as their blood. These men were Balam Quitze, Balam Acab, Mahucutah, and Iqui Balam. They had all the abilities of regular people: they could talk, walk, see, and hear. They also knew everything there was to know beneath the sky. They were infinitely grateful to the gods for having created them. The gods, though, decided to blur their eyes so they could not see everything, but only near, so they were less like the gods themselves and unable to really rival their power. Having thus satisfied themselves of there being no chance of a competition, the gods gave the four first men their respective wives: Cahapaluna, Chomiha, Tzununiha, and Caquixaha. Between them the four couples founded the Quiché people.

What is very interesting here, is that the gods are depicted as having both a clear intention of being recognized and adored as such, and a fear of being somehow overpowered. They also fail in their first attempts at creating the human race as they envision it. This means that they are not depicted as clearly perfect, and eternally infallible, but rather as having at least a semblance of human attributes. They are able to be wrong in their attempts to create something. They are able to feel enough vanity to actively want to be worshiped as the gods that they are, and to want to preserve their status as the most revered and powerful beings in existence. This is something we can also see in other mythologies, such as the Greek and Roman ones, in which the gods are depicted as having many human attributes—including various negative ones.

Kumix: a Hero Who Brings Rain, and the Common Points With the Myth of Quetzalcoatl

Hero tales in Mesoamerica often took the shape of fixed episodes, and therefore repeated themselves to a certain extent between one culture and the other. Such is the case of the ch'orti myth of the Kumix Angel, the rain hero. It has various points of connection with the hero tale of Quetzalcoatl, a popular Aztec tale.

In the case of Quetzalcoatl, he is born connected to the water. He becomes an orphan and is adopted by an old cannibal woman. He must fight his brothers, or alternatively his father's brothers. His father is killed, or has been killed, and he finally succeeds in defeating his father's murderers. He must also look for his father's grave. He gains access to the Underworld. He opens the Maize Mountain and goes on to be a conqueror. These are the basic points of the Quetzalcoatl hero story. There are also important points in the myth of Kumix Angel. Except that, in the case of the myth of Kumix, the story is centered on rainmaking.

Kumix lives with his four older brothers, and one day, as he is in the river bathing to clean a wound in his shin—and there are fish feeding on his blood and flesh—the brothers try to kill him. The way in which they try to kill him varies from version to version: in some they throw him into the river, in some they use a stone to brutally attack him.

Eventually, Kumix is left alone and is able to revive himself. An old cannibal woman adopts him. Here there are also variations as to the details of how they become family. In some versions, the old cannibal woman, the K'ech'uj, hears him sobbing. In other versions, she sees the bloody water, and adopts Kumix because she mistakes that bloody water for her own aborted child.

Up to this point, the myth mentions not only water, but also blood. This is a reference to human sacrifice—which makes full sense when we consider that Mesoamericans sacrificed children to the rain gods.

After some time of having his adoptive mother take whatever he hunts away from him to give to her lover, and upon discovering that they are not his real parents, he kills them both.

After this, Kumix travels to find his mother. She has been taken to the heavens, and he reaches her by being carried by a hummingbird hidden in a guitar. Sadly, she has been left in total poverty by the Bronze King, who took all of her properties; but fortunately her son is able to help. He also manages to multiply the few kernels of maize and beans she has left, and produce fowl. In some versions, his uncle San Lorenzo builds, or rebuilds, his and his mother's house.

Later, he sets out to find those who kidnapped his mother and killed his father within the forest. They also have his father's rainmaking implements with them, and Kumix needs to take them back. He succeeds by facing animal helpers of the Bronze Kings. He also kills the Bronze King himself.

Using his drum and his sword, he begins to create the rain needed by the vegetation to grow and produce thunder and lightning. His brothers try to get to their mother by creating a mountain by which to ascend to the heavens; but Kumix impedes this by destroying the mountain with his lightning. This also takes care of the eagles that were coming down that mountain and posing a threat to humanity. The brothers disobey an order to hide their heads, and become blind as a consequence. They start tearing up, and those tears bring the November drizzles to the region. By the power of Kumix, they become rain priests, and are assigned mountains in the four corners of the world. And so, the December and January rains came to be.

Finally, Kumix is able to find his father's grave, and tries to resurrect him. Unfortunately, he is unable to do so, because a swarm of quails breaks his concentration. He ascends to the sky and he becomes the sun.

There are a couple of salient details in the story of Kumix that may call the reader's attention, and which represent features of the Mesoamerican worldview mentioned in this book. These details are shared by the story of Quetzalcoátl, albeit in a different way; but for the sake of simplicity, it's the case of Kumix that will be mentioned.

In the first place, the myth combines the idea of bringing rain with the idea of the sun. Kumix, being the bringer of rain and the one that becomes the sun, represents both. This may refer to the idea of nature and the circle of life being a singular, unbroken cycle, Everything is somehow related, making nature what it is.

This ties up with the very high importance that Mesoamerican cultures gave to nature in general, and to the sun and the rain in particular. The dynamic between both is beautifully depicted in this myth.

The second detail worth mentioning is the mention of family struggles, loss, and even rivalry. The process Kumix lives is not an easy one: he must overcome obstacles and defeat enemies. This part of the story makes clear that Mesoamerican gods—and, by extension, heroes like Kumix—share many traits with the human race.

CHAPTER 11
MESOAMERICAN LEGACY — LITTLE PIECES OF THE INDIGENOUS MESOAMERICAN PEOPLE IN OUR MODERN-DAY WORLD

Unfortunately, the great Mesoamerican civilizations we have studied in this book no longer exist in the way that they used to. Our modern culture has taken their place, starting with the Spanish conquest. The people alive today that share the ancestry of one of these civilizations, live a very different life from the ones this book has described.

Nevertheless, we can still spot ways in which these great cultures still permeate our world today. This may be true in two different ways: as a means of preserving the indigenous cultures and letting us present-day inhabitants of the world know about them, or as practices, knowledge, or tools that we still use today, although said practices, knowledge or tools, and their use, may have been modified by time and circumstances. In both cases, we have important bonds between modern inhabitants of the American continent and its aboriginal inhabitants.

A Writing System

Among the fascinating cultural achievements of the Mesoamerican civilizations we find their writing system, first developed by the Olmecs. This system was very different from the way we write today, using logograms or glyphs—symbols that represented a whole word or concept—rather than letters to represent sounds as our system does. But pre- hispanic Mesoamerican writings had a very similar function to our present-day writing: to record things in a way that is far more permanent than orally transmitting it from person to person.

Perhaps the main reason why the Measoamerican writing system is so important, is the fact that it serves as a link between our modern world and theirs: many of the things archaeologists know about Mesoamerican indigenous peoples—and, by extension, what we know about them thanks to their investigations—has been transmitted to us by written records.

Architecture and the Pyramids

Another remnant that the great Mesoamerican cultures have left behind them are architectural ones. These peoples acquired highly sophisticated levels of knowledge on subjects such as astrology and mathematics, and this most certainly had a strong impact on the architecture of their cities, which became monumental and complex. The vestiges of them that we can find today tell us fascinating stories of how these cities were, and by extension, how the people inhabiting them viewed the world, and ultimately, lived their lives.

A particular example of this is that of the pyramids, which can still be found in many places in the Mesoamerican region and have even become tourist attractions. The main function of the pyramids was a ceremonial one, and they were truly the maximal expression of these peoples' architectural prowess.

Among the important pyramids of the American continent we can count the following:

- The Cholula Pyramid: located in San Andrés Cholula, in the state of Puebla, in Mexico. It's also known as Tlachihualtepetl, or "hand-made mountain" in the nahuatl tongue. It's devoted to the god Questalcoatl. It was constructed around 900 to 1100, and with a height of around 216,5 ft, it's the highest pyramid in Mexico.

- Pyramid of the Sun and pyramid of the Moon: these pyramids are also located in Mexico. The pyramid of the Sun is just a bit shorter than the Cholula pyramid, at nearly 207 ft, while the pyramid of the moon is a bit shorter, measuring just above 147,5 ft. Both pyramids are located in the city of Teotihuacán.
- Pyramid of Kukulkán: this pyramid is also located in Mexico, specifically in Yucatán, in the south-east. It was built in the Mayan city of Chichén-Itzá, and it's nearly 78,76 ft tall.
- Pyramid of La Danta: this Mayan pyramid is situated in Petén, Guatemala, and it's the highest pyramid in America, with a height of over 236,2 ft. It was constructed in 300 B.C.E.
- Temple of the Bicephalous Snake: with a height very similar to that of the Pyramid of the Sun, this pyramid is located in Tikal, Guatemala.

There is a beautiful legend associated with the Pyramid of the Sun and Moon, and it involves the gods Tecuciztecátl and Nanahuatzin. They both volunteered to carry the light of a new day. They both got ready and prepared their offerings, and in due course made their penitence in the mounts the gods prepared for this purpose, which mounts are today known as the pyramids of the Sun and Moon.

Why the names, "sun" and "moon"? Well, Nanahuatzin would turn into the sun, and Tecuciztecátl, into the moon. The gods were reunited around the divine fire, including our protagonists, and Tecuciztecátl was asked to step into the flames. Sadly, he couldn't endure them, and had to step back, even after trying several times. Meanwhile, when Nanahuetzin was asked to do the same, he was tougher than his companion and endured the fire. Tecuciztecátl tried again, although it was late by now. Both gods ended up transforming into suns, Nanahuatzin first, and then Tecuciztecátl; and since the gods didn't need two suns, they transformed one of them—the second one, Tecuciztécatl—into the moon.

Gastronomy and More: Natural Products and Their Use

One of the great tools a people has to express itself is its food. Mesoamerican civilizations were no exception, and the way they ate can still be enjoyed today.

Avocados, corn, squash, beans, and other products are still part of the day-to-day diet of many inhabitants of the American continent. Chocolate—consumed both as a beverage and as a form of candy—was also part of Mesoamerican diet and is, still today, part of the diet of millions of people, both in the American continent and all over the world. Our modern chewing gum derives from a Mayan product.

But, the natural products the great Mersoamerican people used, and we inherited, are not limited to food. They utilized cotton to make clothing, and so do we today. They also dyed their fabrics with natural products, such as logwood and indigo, and even if our modern products and techniques may be different, the idea still stems from indigenous people.

Agriculture and Medicine: Trusty Techniques to Solve Complex Problems

In order to have all of their crops available, the indigenous Mesoamerican people depended highly on trusty agricultural techniques. They often had to deal with difficult conditions from an agricultural standpoint, such as swampy terrain and tropical rains; and their solutions still prove useful today. For example, the chinampas—which allow crops to be cultivated in lakes by putting a layer of vegetals, mud, and fresh soil thereby creating a patch of cultivable soil, like making some sort of compost—are still used today in Mexico.

They also had techniques which they used to heal the sick and injured, some of which are still applied in our modern day. For example, they helped broken bones to heal with the help of casts, much like what we know today. They also used steam baths, called temazcal, for medical purposes. Steam baths are also a part of our modern world.

Artistic Expressions

Mesoamerican cultures all had a variety of artistic expressions, and some of them are reflected in modern-day Mexican art. From architecture to poetry, sculpture to jewelry, the inspiration has permeated time from pre-hispanic indigenous people to modern-day Mexican and non-Mexican artists. This expands to woodcraft, masks, metallurgy, artistic use of glass, and other similar artistic expressions.

Games of Physical and Mental Skill

As the reader can see by recalling the example of the ball game, games often had a ceremonial significance to the indigenous Mesoamerican peoples. But they also had rules, judges, and spectators. They have permeated actual current-day games played in Mexico.

With time, traditional elements have been getting mixed up with elements coming from Europe, creating the current versions of the games. In Mexico, there is an active concern with the decreasing number of people actually playing these ancestral games, and the Mexican government has been promoting their revitalization among university students even as recently as August of 2021.

Religious Syncretism: When Christianity Meets the Mesoamerican Beliefs

When the Spaniards arrived in America to conquer and to convert the natives to Christianity, their religious teachings did not fall onto a completely blank slate. What they were preaching was received, yes, but received by people with their own view of the world, and their own pre-existing set of beliefs. In the process of being converted to Christianity, the indigenous communities mixed their own beliefs and traditions into the new set of beliefs they were acquiring, remaining faithful to their culture, even if they outwardly conformed to the new religion that was being presented to them.

This mixture between native and foreign religious elements is certainly another way in which we can feel the impact of native Mesoamerican civilizations in our present-day world.

An example of this is the close relationship that certain Christian festivities in certain areas of Mexico, such as Guerrero and Veracruz in the central region of the country, have with the agricultural cycle, a very important part of the aboriginal worldview and a key part of how their very calendar was determined. The agricultural significance of these festivities has much to do with the cycle of sowing, maturing, and reaping of the crops, thereby celebrating the natural cycle of agriculture. Naturally, each of these steps of the cycle is commemorated in the adequate moment of the year, the moment when that particular agricultural step takes place. There are also festivities that celebrate fertility and agriculture in general.

In Xochimilco, Mexico, the Fiesta de la Candelaria—a celebration devoted to the Virgin of la Candelaria which is held in February—has several agricultural references, including the blessing of seeds that are to be planted much later in the year.

In Alto Balsas, also in Mexico, the Carnival that takes place just before Easter is deeply associated with fertility and with corn, a sacred plant.

Festivities such as San Marcos celebrated on April 25 in Santa Cruz, the Holy Cross, which falls on May 3rd, or San Isidro Labrador falling on May 15th are associated in the Mesoamerican region—Mexico, Honduras, and Guatemala—with the petition for rain. Asking the gods for rain, and hopefully getting an adequate amount of it, was deeply important for the native Mesoamerican cultures, dependent as they were on the cycles of Nature to survive. This still shows in today's celebrations. The moment of the year in which these petitions for rains occur, is around May or June, which in the Northern Hemisphere, where Mesoamerica is located, is Spring.

Not all of these festivities are celebrated everywhere in Mesoamerica, but whichever of them is actually celebrated, the people ask for rain as their ancestors would have done. In some regions of Mexico, such as Morelos, the petition for rain may be done a bit later in the year, for example during the Día de San Juan (Day of St. John, June 24). In this region, late June to early July is when the sowing season ends, so it's a good time to pray for a good year for the crops.

Continuing with the agricultural cycle, the maturation of corn is very present as a part of the religious celebrations that take place in August, such as San Salvador on August 6 or the Assumption of the Virgin on August 15.

Finally, the reaping season takes place in November, and the Día de los Muertos (Day of the dead), celebrated in Mexico on November 2, celebrates the reaping at the same time it honors the ancestors.

Indigenous Voices in the Modern World: the Example of the Changes in Education Brought About by the Zapatista Movement in Mexico

Being home to many of the great civilizations discussed in this book, Mexico is currently home to many people with cultural ties to some of these civilizations. These people were not always considered in their unique needs: but they had, and still have today, a voice. That voice demanding their identity be recognized and respected is certainly a powerful way in which the Mesoamerican cultures can still be felt in our modern world. And that voice is all the more active in those locations in which the disconnect between the perceived needs of the people identifying with some indigenous people and the reality they face is great.

The Zapatista movement—starting in 1994— made this known and urged the Mexican authorities to address the issue of indigenous identity. A good example of this is found in education. Let the reader bear in mind that, when the Zapatista Movement started, Mexican education did not cater to the country's cultural diversity, treating everyone as basically belonging to the same cultural background. This explains why the Zapatista movement had education as one of their first and most basic demands.

As an example of the Zapatista influence in education, a project called the Proyecto del Educador Comunitario Indígena (Communitary Indigenous Educator Project; PECI for its initials in Spanish) was created as a response to the Zapatista demands. The idea was to offer the community an education that could be actually considered "indigenous", meaning taught by teachers who identified as belonging to an indigenous group and who were fluent in the language of that indigenous culture. The idea was to allow the actual community to decide the main guidelines in which the education given was to be based, while at the same time allowing new schools to appear in places where there were none, therefore allowing more children to be educated.

Another example of how Zapatista ideals had

a concrete impact on Mexican education is the fact that the Zapatistas, specifically the Ejército Zapatista de Liberación Nacional (Zapatista National Liberation Army, EZLN for its initials in Spanish), negotiated with the Mexican authorities to aim for an education that catered specifically to the cultural needs of the people being educated. These negotiations culminated on February 16 1996, with the signing of the Acuerdo de San Andrés, or San Andrés Agreement, which reflected the Zapatista concerns and demands.

CONCLUSION

The Aboriginal Mesoamerican Civilizations Had Some Great Features

While very different from their European counterparts, aboriginal Measoamericans were not any less civilized than their European counterparts, despite what the Europeans themselves thought about the subject. For all the discussion the conquering Spaniards had among themselves about whether or not the aboriginals even had souls of their own, or about whether or not they were even human, they could not help but be quite impressed by the sophisticated cultural level exhibited by the natives. That cultural level was not only what those who defended the natives being human used as arguments; but also a reason for the conquistadors to believe in the conversion of the natives to the "true faith" as a feasible feat.

Archaeological remains show us civilizations

with a really advanced grasp of several subjects, from how to solve the practicalities of cultivating their food in conditions that were far from ideal—as exemplified by the chinampas used even today to make viable soil out of lakes, to mathematics, and astrology—as exemplified by their calendar. Their writing system also put them above other cultures, allowing them to communicate in a way that was much more durable than oral speech. Their social structure was also complex, rivaling that of any European country, with differentiated social classes, nobility, and rulers on top of it, priests with highly specialized tasks, and commoners like you could find anywhere else. Moctezuma was just as great a sovereign in his realm as the King of Spain was in his own.

Their religious beliefs and mythology are also fascinating, and they show us an understanding of nature, and even of death as a part of life, that we seem to have forgotten amidst the chaos that is modern life. The careful way the great Mesoamerican cities were constructed are a testimony to the utmost importance given to detail, to religion, and to the spiritual world in general. Among the many architectural achievements of those cities, the pyramids, those great impressive ceremonial centers that could reach tens of meters in height, deserve a special mention as a true demonstration of their ingenuity.

The Aboriginal Mesoamerican Civilizations Are Important Even Today

Even though the great Mesoamerican civilizations do not exist anymore today like they used to, they still live on through many aspects of modern life in the Mesoamerican region. Starting from the fact that there are many people today that identify as belonging to one of these indigenous groups—as evidenced by the existence of such a thing as the Zapatista movement in Mexico—and continuing with architectural wonders such as the pyramids, marvels of practical ingenuity still useful today such as the chinampas that help make agriculture easier, and wonderful cultural expressions such as the religious syncretism present Mexico and in the rest of Mesoamerica. Even the way people inhabiting the Mesoamerican region eat is heavily influenced by these fascinating cultures, and in today's hyper connected world, this influence can be felt not only in Mesoamerica, but all around the world.

Whether we may even think of it or not, the people who inhabited the world before us helped make it into what it is today, and this is evident in the case of Mesoamerica. That fact alone is more than enough to make the aboriginal inhabitants of the region important even to this day. The very distinct way in which they still show up in our modern life, every concret print of those civilizations that we can find, is just one more reason adding to that importance.

The reader, having finished this book, should be able to understand this importance and appreciate it as it deserves. He or she should also be able to extend this appreciation to every civilization, every people, and every historical event that shaped our present.

The Aboriginal Mesoamerican Civilizations Are Made Reachable To You by This Book

In its introduction, this book promised the reader an immersive journey into the world of Mesoamerican aboriginal civilizations. Firstly, this book has provided the reader with an accessible source of information, written in a way that is both engaging and easy to understand. Both characteristics are essential for the book to achieve its purpose of communicating knowledge. Of course, what is not understood is not really communicated: therefore this book was written specifically to be easily readable. But also, to properly communicate something, the information given must resonate at some level with the person it is given to, and that makes making this book an agreeable read just as important as making it an easily comprehensible one.

It has done so by a careful writing process, rooted in the understanding that information is just as useful as its capacity to reach the people it's aimed at. Knowledge does not have real value until it's properly communicated, through a message—in this case, a written text in the form of a book—that is both clear and engaging. This book was written with that principle always at the forefront, and is thus able to deliver on its promise.

Secondly, the book has also provided material that allows the reader to immerse him or herself into the world of these fascinating civilizations, mysterious as they may sometimes seem to us contemporary inhabitants of the world. It has done so because it's the result of a careful study of several sources, which allows for a wide look at the material that is being presented. This, in turn, allows the reader a wealth of information that can help him or her get a very clear mental image of the world the book is depicting, which is where the immersive experience stems from.

All of this matters, because a very high-quality book is the only result acceptable to History Brought Alive. Being curious and informed makes living a much more exciting experience, and History Brought Alive strives to give its readers precisely that sense of curiosity and a reliable source of information to placate it with.

REFERENCES

Adams, R. E., & MacLeod, M. J. (Eds.). (2000). The Cambridge history of the Native Peoples of the Americas (Vol. 2). Cambridge University Press. https://assets.cambridge.org/97805213/51652/sample/9780521351652wsn01.pdf

Alconini, S., & Covey, R. A. (Eds.). (2018). *The Oxford handbook of the Incas.* Oxford University Press. https://scholar.google.com/scholar?hl=es&as_sdt=0%2C5&q=oxford+handbook+of+the+incas&btnG=#d=gs_cit&t=1682911145247&u=%2Fscholar%3Fq%3Dinfo%3Adj5YnAKxuPsJ%3Ascholar.google.com%2F%26output%3Dcite%26scirp%3D0%26hl%3Des

Armillas, P. (1945). *Los dioses de Teotihuacan* (Vol. 6, pp. 35-61). Impresores Best.

Bauer, B. S. (1996). *The Development of the Inca State.* Google Books. University of Texas Press. https://books.google.cl/books?hl=es&lr=&id=emOMCgAAQBAJ&oi=fnd&pg=PR11&dq=inca+hierarchy&ots=oLR-5OUTcx&sig=gitZafvsVnkhvozMj1BkRInWvgI&redir_esc=y#v=onepage&q=inca%20hierarchy&f=false

Benítez, E. L. B. (2014). *Symbolism and Use of Maize in Pre-Hispanic and Colonial Religious Imagery in Mexico.* 53 TECHNICAL, 117.

Bernal, I. (1969). *The Olmec World.* In Google Books. University of California Press. https://books.google.cl/books?hl=es&lr=&id=BIqdIYufqmgC&oi=fnd&pg=PA1&dq=olmec+religious+beliefs&ots=qM6EemNpow&sig=lcdGN-oCt-eM3P-C7ftIGsir9Ro&redir_esc=y#v=onepage&q=olmec%20religious%20beliefs&f=false

Bible Gateway. (s.f.). https://www.biblegateway.com/passage/?search=Genesis%202&version=NIV, s.f.

Blanton, R. E., Kowalewski, S. A., Feinman, G. M., &

Finsten, L. M. (1993). *Ancient Mesoamerica: A Comparison of Change in Three Regions*. In Google Books. Cambridge University Press. https://books.google.cl/books?hl=es&lr=&id=bwGH fuqnMeUC&oi=fnd&pg=PR5&dq=mesoamerica+key +facts&ots=AxcFSgeFJU&sig=IsF2EZ-x5_uy6OkR6fks_GT6k6Y&redir_esc=y#v=onepage &q=mesoamerica%20key%20facts&f=false

Braakhuis, E., & Hull, K. (2014). *Pluvial Aspects of the Mesoamerican Culture Hero. The "Kumix Angel" of the Ch'orti'Mayans and Other Rain-Bringing Heroes*. Anthropos, 109(2), 449-466.

Broda, J. (2003). *La ritualidad mesoamericana y los procesos de sincretismo y reelaboración simbólica después de la conquista*. Graffylia, 2, 14-28.

Calleman, C. J. (2004). *The Mayan Calendar and the Transformation of Consciousness*. In Google Books. Simon and Schuster. https://books.google.cl/books?hl=es&lr=&id=N10o DwAAQBAJ&oi=fnd&pg=PT9&dq=mayan+calendar &ots=u3Aemn0gsj&sig=oeAyxfkxQ7Soa5YfH5dsEzh Tkro&redir_esc=y#v=onepage&q=mayan%20calend ar&f=false

Carrasco, D. (2013). *Religions of Mesoamerica: Second Edition*. In Google Books. Waveland Press. https://books.google.cl/books?hl=es&lr=&id=mc-rAAAAQBAJ&oi=fnd&pg=PR3&dq=mesoamerica+k ey+facts&ots=z35qBez5Ly&sig=-HpiTzGuPHFsfzTgzVNLzES1Wwo&redir_esc=y#v= onepage&q=mesoamerica%20key%20facts&f=false

Cobo, F. B., & Hamilton, R. (1990). *Inca Religion and Customs*. In Google Books. University of Texas Press. https://books.google.cl/books?hl=es&lr=&id=FlBpZ DF7-XUC&oi=fnd&pg=PR7&dq=inca+empire+religion& ots=zmSqQ6cdOu&sig=TwUdURTxbgtKqw4u9hrdE cftfsE&redir_esc=y#v=onepage&q=inca%20empire %20religion&f=false

Collis, M. (1999). *Cortés and Montezuma*. In Google

Books. New Directions Publishing. https://books.google.cl/books?hl=es&lr=&id=0fpaP u4xkFUC&oi=fnd&pg=PA21&dq=hernan+cortes+an d+montezuma&ots=paGqgo8WZm&sig=bhqfnBDDf 3eP_1vKE84PZPnZYMA&redir_esc=y#v=onepage& q=hernan%20cortes%20and%20montezuma&f=fals e

Creamer, W. (1987). *Mesoamerica as a Concept: An Archaeological View from Central America*. Latin American Research Review, 22(1), 35–62. https://doi.org/10.1017/s0023879100016423

Cultura Teotihuacana - Información, historia, religión y aportes. (n.d.). https://concepto.de/cultura-teotihuacana/

Cyphers, A. (1996). *Reconstructing Olmec Life at San Lorenzo*. Olmec art of ancient Mexico, 61-71.

Dreiss, M. L., & Greenhill, S. (2008). *Chocolate: Pathway to the Gods*. In Google Books. University of Arizona Press. https://books.google.cl/books?hl=es&lr=&id=tEFsZ uKRbNcC&oi=fnd&pg=PP11&dq=mesoamerican+go ds&ots=5yevuWy6_w&sig=x7mhEokODVN6-sQ4jc6JrxJGfxg&redir_esc=y#v=onepage&q=mesoa merican%20gods&f=false

Flannery, K. V., & Marcus, J. (1976). *Formative Oaxaca and the Zapotec Cosmos: The interactions of ritual and human ecology are traced in this interpretation of a prehistoric settlement in highland Mexico*. American Scientist, 64(4), 374-383.

Florescano, E. (1997). *Sobre la naturaleza de los dioses de Mesoamérica* (pp. 71–95). Anthropologica, 15(15),.

Florescano, E. (2002). The Myth of Quetzalcoatl. In Google Books. JHU Press. https://books.google.cl/books?hl=es&lr=&id=3HDp rRxXsGsC&oi=fnd&pg=PP15&dq=quetzalc%C3%B3 atl+the+god&ots=hW7seXu65A&sig=fKamv6CVvdil -

ow3NOSWKlRStfo&redir_esc=y#v=onepage&q=qu

etzalc%C3%B3atl%20the%20god&f=false

Gutiérrez Narváez, R. (2006). Impactos del zapatismo en la escuela: análisis de la dinámica educativa indígena en Chiapas (1994-2004). Liminar, 4(1), 92-111.

Hassig, R. (1988). Aztec Warfare: Imperial Expansion and Political Control. In Google Books. University of Oklahoma Press. https://books.google.cl/books?hl=es&lr=&id=7M1o 9g8MARgC&oi=fnd&pg=PR13&dq=aztec+pilli&ots= FriHw28qP3&sig=M6OnCpaUWmyFzUz-lyUGnPxmI8o&redir_esc=y#v=onepage&q=aztec%2 opilli&f=false

HDT. (n.d.). Pep.ieepo.oaxaca.gob.mx. Retrieved April 9, 2023, from http://pep.ieepo.oaxaca.gob.mx/recursos/interactiv o/PA6_HI_B3_OA_20365/informacionfase5.html# :~:text=Por%20eso%2C%20entre%20las%20herenc ias

Headrick, A. (2007). *The Teotihuacan Trinity: The Sociopolitical Structure of an Ancient Mesoamerican City*. In Google Books. University of Texas Press. https://books.google.cl/books?hl=es&lr=&id=15kty Fb4JvgC&oi=fnd&pg=PR7&dq=teotihuacan+social+ structure&ots=wQBGiSbKpj&sig=r3d_iUybmTNWT mNIHocN6sjah9I&redir_esc=y#v=onepage&q=teot ihuacan%20social%20structure&f=false

Honore, P. (2007). *In Search of Quetzalcoatl: The Mysterious Heritage of South American Civilization*. In Google Books. Adventures Unlimited Press. https://books.google.cl/books?hl=es&lr=&id=mNv4 ofH2Mk8C&oi=fnd&pg=PA13&dq=quetzalc%C3%B 3atl+went+away&ots=ghCi-B9g2K&sig=pCtdTx-btATr8pfolTjc3M_VgXQ&redir_esc=y#v=onepage& q=quetzalc%C3%B3atl%20went%20away&f=false

Kelley, D. H., & Kerr, K. A. (1973). M*ayan astronomy and astronomical glyphs*. In Mesoamerican Writing Systems: A Conference at Dumbarton Oaks, October 30th and 31st, 1971. Dumbarton Oaks. https://books.google.cl/books?hl=es&lr=&id=I9xnY

2UTWpgC&oi=fnd&pg=PA179&dq=mayan+astrono
my&ots=Bil_0-
4pnx&sig=A_bCdRxcVxQ1okDdcU_QjOo6L2I&redi
r_esc=y#v=onepage&q=mayan%20astronomy&f=fa
lse

La Leyenda de las Pirámides de Teotihuacán. (2019,
November 7). Universidad de Oriente Puebla.
https://www.uo.edu.mx/blog/la-leyenda-de-las-
pir%C3%A1mides-de-
teotihuac%C3%A1n#:~:text=Pir%C3%A1mide%20de
l%20Sol%3A%20con%20cinco

Lipovac, N., & Gradečki, N. (2018). *Mayan Cities of
Yucatan*. Prostor, 26(2 (56)), 282–295.
https://doi.org/10.31522/p.26.2(56).6

Marcus, J., & Flannery, K. V. (1994). *Ancient Zapotec
ritual and religion: an application of the direct
historical approach*. The ancient mind: elements of
cognitive archaeology, 55-74.

*Mesoamérica: información, religión, aportes y
características*. (n.d.). Https://Humanidades.com/.
Retrieved April 9, 2023, from
https://humanidades.com/mesoamerica/#:~:text=E
ntre%20los%20aportes%20m%C3%A1s%20importa
ntes

Miller, M. E. (1989). *The ballgame*. Record of the Art
Museum, Princeton University, 48(2), 22-31.

Millon, R. (1991). *The last years of Teotihuacán
dominance*. In N. Yoffee & G. Cowgill (Eds.), Google
Books. University of Arizona Press.
https://books.google.cl/books?hl=es&lr=&id=L5kw
EAAAQBAJ&oi=fnd&pg=PA102&dq=teotihuacan+s
ocial+structure&ots=maHAh9_0m-
&sig=4K9KokjMIhvuC6Q1q6a5y77kFyA&redir_esc=
y#v=onepage&q=teotihuacan%20social%20structur
e&f=false

Mitla, Oaxaca. (2016, July 27). Arqueología Mexicana.
https://arqueologiamexicana.mx/mexico-
antiguo/mitla-oaxaca

Nichols, D. L., & Rodríguez-Alegría, E. (2016). *The Oxford*

Handbook of the Aztecs. In Google Books. Oxford University Press. https://books.google.cl/books?hl=es&lr=&id=0chjD QAAQBAJ&oi=fnd&pg=PA201&dq=tenochtitl%C3% A1n+aztec+city&ots=7ulgmMeIa4&sig=rGN-mhtYhU6tjO9ESPmusyl-IpI&redir_esc=y#v=onepage&q=tenochtitl%C3%A1 n%20aztec%20city&f=false

Nuevos e interesantes descubrimientos en la gran pirámide de Cholula, en México. (2023, February 10). Historia.nationalgeographic.com.es. https://historia.nationalgeographic.com.es/a/nuevo s-e-interesantes-descubrimientos-en-la-gran-piramide-de-cholula-en-mexico_19116

Pasztory, E. (1974). *The Iconography of the Teotihuacan Tlaloc.* In Google Books. Dumbarton Oaks. https://books.google.cl/books?hl=es&lr=&id=L0QC lI2QOwQC&oi=fnd&pg=PA3&dq=tlaloc+god&ots=q PBZ5AJoub&sig=ugjs-kpiqYGd0l-IrYxgXOsdtbo&redir_esc=y#v=onepage&q=tlaloc% 20god&f=false

Pharo, L. K. (2013). *The Ritual Practice of Time: Philosophy and Sociopolitics of Mesoamerican Calendars.* In Google Books. BRILL. https://books.google.cl/books?hl=es&lr=&id=SHZf AgAAQBAJ&oi=fnd&pg=PR5&dq=mesoamerican+ri tuals&ots=2GZL4P4U7p&sig=u1rNQHsaXp-bc_P8A2SkokMmBxg&redir_esc=y#v=onepage&q= mesoamerican%20rituals&f=false

Pool, C. (2007). *Olmec Archaeology and Early Mesoamerica.* In Google Books. Cambridge University Press. https://books.google.cl/books?hl=es&lr=&id=hXmf pro8JPUC&oi=fnd&pg=PA5&dq=olmecs&ots=tTtwi vU_Wn&sig=UHotIZihI7yaxndjpN59msuU2yU&red ir_esc=y#v=onepage&q=olmecs&f=false

Popol Vuh: sacred book of the Quiché Maya people. (A. J. Christenson, Trans.). (2012).

Prescott, W. H. (1873). *History of the Conquest of Mexico.*

In Google Books. [J.B.] Lippincott. https://books.google.cl/books?hl=es&lr=&id=S2TU ddcBslEC&oi=fnd&pg=PR23&dq=history+of+the+c onquest+%22hernando+cort%C3%A9s%22&ots=8P bMLXgYJ4&sig=toS2p1K4gZdxdmZisdwkmu1yWp4 &redir_esc=y#v=onepage&q=history%20of%20the %20conquest%20%22hernando%20cort%C3%A9s% 22&f=false

Read, K. A., & Gonzalez, J. J. (2002). *Mesoamerican Mythology: A Guide to the Gods, Heroes, Rituals, and Beliefs of Mexico and Central America*. In Google Books. OUP USA. https://books.google.cl/books?hl=es&lr=&id=Yo53 PeFmS5UC&oi=fnd&pg=PR11&dq=mesoamerican+ gods&ots=pT9L3hhZyj&sig=Q5ptf1ee_jW1sFydrbL NrwPJxwo&redir_esc=y#v=onepage&q=mesoameri can%20gods&f=false

Regas, R., & Cañagueral, A. (2017). *The Secrets of Ancient Ritual Sites: The Citadel of Machu Picchu and Stonehenge*T. In Google Books. Cavendish Square Publishing, LLC. https://books.google.cl/books?hl=es&lr=&id=uCpm DwAAQBAJ&oi=fnd&pg=PP1&dq=machu+picchu+ book&ots=lt8kSDNHIQ&sig=SGK-3WQ9KXhnu2xmpxzpIttLaKg&redir_esc=y#v=one page&q=machu%20picchu%20book&f=false)

Richardson, G. (2018). *Machu Picchu*. In Google Books. Weigl Publishers. https://books.google.cl/books?hl=es&lr=&id=Rb62 DwAAQBAJ&oi=fnd&pg=PA4&dq=machu+picchu+ book&ots=F_esGocs56&sig=8NokosuWUYMDNDa QEEVCnIG63PQ&redir_esc=y#v=onepage&q=mach u%20picchu%20book&f=false

Robb, M. (2017). *Teotihuacan: City of Water, City of Fire*. In Google Books. Univ of California Press. https://books.google.cl/books?hl=es&lr=&id=PDEy DwAAQBAJ&oi=fnd&pg=PA1&dq=teotihuacan+reli gion&ots=KEqBswdr5X&sig=-d__6-zb-FhQGok-ezTJ8oMi7Do&redir_esc=y#v=onepage&q=teotihua

can%20religion&f=false

Robles, B., Flores, J., Martínez, J. L., & Herrera, P. (2018). *The Chinampa: An Ancient Mexican Sub-Irrigation System*. Irrigation and Drainage, 68(1). https://doi.org/10.1002/ird.2310

Shane III, O. C. (1984). *Cenote of sacrifice: Maya treasures from the sacred well at Chichén Itzá*. University of Texas Press.

Smith, M. (2006). *Aztec culture: an overview*. https://eclass.uoa.gr/modules/document/file.php/S PANLL152/%CE%A5%CF%83%CF%84_%CE%9A% CE%BB%CE%B1%CF%83%CE%B9%CE%BA%CE% AE/%CE%91%CE%B6%CF%84%CE%AD%CE%BA% CE%BF%CE%B9/%CE%91%CE%B6%CF

Taube, K. A., & Oaks, D. (2004). *Olmec Art at Dumbarton Oaks*. In Google Books. Dumbarton Oaks. https://books.google.cl/books?hl=es&lr=&id=_bjLI FFJjeoC&oi=fnd&pg=PR9&dq=olmec+art+style&ot s=1YYqnICM1e&sig=FP7b6iC2NJz5h76esf4tlF0tAqo &redir_esc=y#v=onepage&q=olmec%20art%20style &f=false4%CE%AD%CE%BA%CE%BF%CE%B92.pd f

Turismo, S. de. (n.d.). *San Pablo Villa de Mitla, Oaxaca*. Gob.mx. Retrieved April 16, 2023, from https://www.gob.mx/sectur/es/articulos/san-pablo-villa-mitla-oaxaca

Univision. (n.d.). *Las pirámides más importantes de América*. Univision. Retrieved April 11, 2023, from https://www.univision.com/explora/las-piramides-mas-importantes-de-america

Winter, M. (1994). *Monte Albán. Domestic ritual in ancient mesoamerica*, 67.

FREE BONUS FROM HBA: EBOOK BUNDLE

Greetings!

First of all, thank you for reading our books. As fellow passionate readers of History and Mythology, we aim to create the very best books for our readers.

Now, we invite you to join our VIP list. As a welcome gift, we offer the History & Mythology Ebook Bundle below for free. Plus you can be the first to receive new books and exclusives! <u>Remember it's 100% free to join.</u>

Simply scan the QR code to join.

OTHER BOOKS BY
HISTORY BROUGHT ALIVE

Available now in Ebook, Paperback, Hardcover, and Audiobook in all regions.

NORSE
MAGIC & RUNES
HISTORY BROUGHT ALIVE

NORSE MYTHOLOGY,
VIKINGS, MAGIC &
RUNES
3 books in 1
HISTORY BROUGHT ALIVE

NORSE
MYTHOLOGY
HISTORY BROUGHT ALIVE

ANCIENT
EGYPT
HISTORY BROUGHT ALIVE

GREEK
MYTHOLOGY
HISTORY BROUGHT ALIVE

NORSE
PAGANISM
FOR BEGINNERS
HISTORY BROUGHT ALIVE

GREEK, MESOPOTAMIA,
EGYPT & ROME
HISTORY BROUGHT ALIVE

MYTHOLOGY OF
MESOPOTAMIA
HISTORY BROUGHT ALIVE

JAPANESE
HISTORY
HISTORY BROUGHT ALIVE

For Kids:

MYTHOLOGY FOR KIDS
Explore Timeless Tales, Characters, History, & Legendary Stories from Around the World. Norse, Celtic, Roman, Greek, Egypt & Many More
HISTORY BROUGHT ALIVE

NORSE MYTHOLOGY FOR KIDS
Legendary Stories, Quests & Timeless Tales From Norse Folklore. The Myths, Sagas & Epics of The Gods, Immortals, Magic Creatures, Vikings & More
HISTORY BROUGHT ALIVE

THE HISTORY OF ENGLAND FOR KIDS
From Anglo-Saxons to Tudors & Modern Times - A Fun-filled Journey Through Centuries of English History, Kings & Queens
HISTORY BROUGHT ALIVE

MESOAMERICAN HISTORY & MYTHOLOGY

We sincerely hope you enjoyed our new book *"Mesoamerican History & Mythology"*. We would greatly appreciate your feedback with an honest review at the place of purchase.

First and foremost, we are always looking to grow and improve as a team. It is reassuring to hear what works, as well as receive constructive feedback on what should improve. Second, starting out as an unknown author is exceedingly difficult, and Amazon reviews go a long way toward making the journey out of anonymity possible. Please take a few minutes to write an honest review.

Best regards,
History Brought Alive
http://historybroughtalive.com/